GW00580140

THE GREEK ISLANDS
Genius Loci

View of Naxos island seen through the monumental doorway of the Archaic temple.
Thomas Hope (1769-1831) Watercolour, 44 x 29 cm. Benaki Museum, Inv. No. 27375.
© 2010 Benaki Museum, Athens.

Author's acknowledgements

This series of twenty books covering the Aegean Islands is the fruit of many years of solitary dedication to a job difficult to accomplish given the extent of the subject matter and the geography involved. My belief throughout has been that only what is seen with the eyes can trustfully be written about; and to that end I have attempted to walk, ride, drive, climb, sail and swim these Islands in order to inspect everything talked about here. There will be errors in this text inevitably for which, although working in good faith, I alone am responsible. Notwithstanding, I am confident that these are the best, most clearly explanatory and most comprehensive artistic accounts currently available of this vibrant and historically dense corner of the Mediterranean.

Professor Robin Barber, author of the last, general, *Blue Guide to Greece* (based in turn on Stuart Rossiter's masterful text of the 1960s), has been very generous with support and help; and I am also particularly indebted to Charles Arnold for meticulously researched factual data on the Islands and for his support throughout this project. I could not have asked for a more saintly and helpful editor, corrector and indexer than Judy Tither. Efi Stathopoulou, Peter Cocconi, Marc René de Montalembert, Valentina Ivancich, William Forrester and Geoffrey Cox have all given invaluable help; and I owe a large debt of gratitude to John and Jay Rendall for serial hospitality and encouragement. For companionship on many journeys, I would like to thank a number of dear friends: Graziella Seferiades, Ivan Tabares, Matthew Kidd, Martin Leon, my group of Louisianan friends, and my brother Iain— all of whose different reactions to and passions for Greece have been a constant inspiration.

This work is dedicated with admiration and deep affection to Ivan de Jesus Tabares-Valencia who, though a native of the distant Andes mountains, from the start understood the profound spiritual appeal of the Aegean world.

McGILCHRIST'S GREEK ISLANDS

7. THE ARGO-SARONIC ISLANDS

GENIUS LOCI PUBLICATIONS
London

McGilchrist's Greek Islands The Argo-Saronic Islands
First edition

Published by Genius Loci Publications
54 Eccleston Road, London W13 0RL

Nigel McGilchrist © 2010
Nigel McGilchrist has asserted his moral rights.

All rights reserved. No part of this publication may be reproduced or used
by any means without the permission of the publisher.

ISBN 978-1-907859-06-9

A CIP catalogue record of this book is available from the British Library.

The author and publisher cannot accept responsibility or liability for
information contained herein, this being in some cases difficult to verify
and subject to change.

Layout and copy-editing by Judy Tither

Cover design by Kate Buckle

Maps and plans by Nick Hill Design

Printed and bound in Great Britain by TJ International Ltd, Padstow, Cornwall

The island maps in this series are based on the cartography of
Terrain Maps
Karneadou 4, 106 75 Athens, Greece
T: +30 210 609 5759, Fx: +30 210 609 5859
terrain@terrainmaps.gr
www.terrainmaps.gr

This book is one of twenty which comprise the complete, detailed
manuscript which the author prepared for the *Blue Guide: Greece,
the Aegean Islands* (2010), and on which the *Blue Guide* was
based. Some of this text therefore appears in the *Blue Guide*.

CONTENTS

Aegina

N

0 1 2 3km

Vaghia

Radioactive
Spring

Temple of
Aphaia

Mesagros

Aghia Marina

Souvala

Kondos

Vathy

Palaiochora

Ag Nektarios

Panaghia Theotokos
Chrysoleontissa

Portes

Taxiarchis

Kazantzakis
House

Nekropolis

Ag Theodori
(Omorphi
Ekklesia)

Panaghia
Phaneromeni

Pachia
Rachi

Sanctuary of
Zeus Hellanios

+531
Mt Oros

Sfendouri

Kapralos
Museum

Prophitis
Elias Bay

Verdika

Plakakia
Lighthouse

Kolones
Aegina

Moni

Metopi

Chalikiáda
Bay

Skala

Megalochóri
(Mylos)

Metochi

Angistri

Limenaria

Aponisos

Dorousa

AEGINA
&
ANGISTRI

The memorable profile of the island with its conical peak at Mount Oros to the south, becomes familiar long before you ever visit Aegina: it is visible from the Acropolis of Athens, from Piraeus, from the road to Corinth, and from virtually any side by land, air or sea, as you leave or arrive in Athens. That was Aegina's problem: it was too near to Athens. And its early commercial strength, marine power and economic wealth—in some respects, greater than that of Athens in the 6th century BC—had to be eliminated if Athens were to grow as she wished to do. The island was, in Pericles's memorable phrase, 'the eyesore of the Piraeus'. Already by the middle of the 5th century BC Aegina had been reduced by Athens to a clerurchy with no independence and only the faint memory of its past pre-eminence. In modernity—as if by an irony of destiny—Aegina once again preceded Athens as the capital city of a partially liberated Greece in 1826, minting the first coins of modern Greece, just as it may have been the first to mint silver coins in Ancient Greece in the 6th century BC.

That a place as lovely as Aegina should be so close to Athens (a little over 20km as the crow flies) comes as a surprise. And there is much on the island to detain the visitor. Its archaeological remains—the well-preserved Temple of Aphaia and the ancient site of Kolona—are amongst the most interesting and important in the Aegean; there are also impressive later remains of a sanctuary of Zeus below Mount Oros. Deliberately hidden from the unwanted attentions of piracy in the centre of the island is the deserted site of Palaiochora, which was the capital of the island during the Byzantine period; its many scattered churches with painted interiors constitute a treasurehouse of Byzantine painting. Equally hidden—this time in the outskirts of the main town—is the tiny painted church of the Aghii Theodori. Even the town centre of Aegina itself is lively and interesting, and has some elegant streets with neoclassical houses.

The cultivated landscape of the island is also quite particular—characterised by the many groves of pistachio trees for which the island is famous: in the valley of Kondós where they combine with olive trees and with dense pines above, the effect is of great beauty. A more rugged beauty is offered by the climb to the summit of Mount Oros (531 m) which provides the best all-round panorama anywhere of the Saronic Gulf and the mountainous coasts of Attica and of the Peloponnese. Aegina may be small, but it is full of variety. Communications are quick and easy between the island and Piraeus and Athens: the contrast with them could not be greater.

HISTORY AND LEGEND

Aegina's history is ancient and complex; the island has frequently been a protagonist in Greek history, both ancient and modern. In legend, Aegina was a daughter of the river-divinity Asopos; she was kidnapped by the enamoured Zeus, brought to the island and had a son, Aiacus or Aiakos, by him. Later Aiacus, as king, changed the name of the island from 'Oenone' (the name of a nymph) or 'Oenopia' ('wine-producing') to Aegina, in honour of his mother. In recognition of his unbending fairness, he was considered to be one of the three judges of the Underworld. Archaeological evidence shows that the island was inhabited from late Neolithic times (4th millennium BC), and was apparently subject to different invasions and colonisations throughout its prehistory: early Helladic invaders of Lycian origin at first, a Bronze Age people of Aeolian descent in the 2nd millennium BC, Achaean settlers in c. 1400 BC beginning a period of Mycenaean occupation, and Dorian invaders, at the end of the 2nd millennium BC, who brought the Thessalian cult of Zeus *Hellanios* to the island.

Herodotus (Bk. VIII, 46) states that Aegina was re-colonised from Epidauros on the mainland opposite, probably around 950 BC. The infertile soil combined with so strategic a geographical position spurred the inhabitants to maritime enterprise. At the end of the 8th century BC, Aegina enjoyed parity with its fellow members (who were seven of the largest cities in Greece) in the prestigious Calaurian League, centred at the nearby sanctuary of *Calauria* on Poros. By the 7th century BC, the Aeginetan navy held first place in the Hellenic world, plying trade from the Black Sea to Egypt, where the island participated in the founding (c. 630 BC) of the important Greek trading station of Naucratis in the Nile delta (Herodotus II, 178). According to Strabo (VIII, 6. 16) Aeginetans are said to have colonised Umbria in Italy, an assertion given some credibility by a 6th century BC dedication found at Gravisca in Etruria (the port of today's Tarquinia) by Aegina's wealthiest and most famous merchant, Sostratos. Thucydides (V, 53) describes the harbour of Aegina as being crowded with merchant ships. The island was noted for pottery and especially for the quality of its bronze-founding. It was probably the first city in Greece to mint its own coins in the mid 6th century: they were in silver, with the image of a turtle on the obverse.

The Persian invasions of Greece put the island in a difficult position because of the importance to it of its commercial relations with Asia Minor. But at the Battle of Salamis in 480 BC, where the Aeginetans were acknowledged to have fought the best of all the Greeks (Herodotus VIII, 93), they atoned for their ambiguity during the First Persian War: the battle marked the zenith of their power. Aegina's wealth and naval strength had long excited the jealousy of Athens, whose own port of Piraeus was marked by the island's blocking presence. Hostilities between the two, and a simmering naval war that had dragged on for nearly 50 years, ended with the forcible incorporation of Aegina into the Athenian Empire (paying a high 30 talent annual tribute) in 458/7 BC (Thucydides I, 108). Pindar (who may have been befriended by the aristocracy of the island) reproaches and warns Athens for her harsh treatment of Aegina in his *Eighth Pythian* ode; but Athens was to go further, and in 431 BC she expelled the Aeginetan rich and ruling classes from their island and settled it with Athenians—effectively terminating the island's independent history. It passed with the rest of Greece to Macedon and afterwards to Attalos of Pergamon. In 133 BC it was bequeathed to Rome in the will of Attalos III. By 45 BC it was referred to as desolate and abandoned by Cicero (*Epistolae ad familiares* IV, 5).

Aegina was a joint bishopric with Keos (Kea) in Byzantine times. Paul of Aegina, celebrated for a treatise of medicine and surgery, was born on the island in the 7th century AD. Saracen raids in the 9th century forced the inhabitants to abandon Kolona and establish a new island capital inland at today's Palaiochora. After 1204 the island was a personal fief of Venetian and Catalan (Fadrique and de Caopena) families, until it passed to the republic of Venice in 1451. It was captured and devastated by Khaireddin Barbarossa in 1537. The island was repopulated with Albanians. Again pillaged and recaptured for Venice by Morosini in 1654, it became one of the last Venetian strongholds in the east, being ceded to the Turks only in 1718. In 1826 the city of Aegina was the de facto seat of government of a partly liberated Greece, under the guidance of Ioannis Capodistrias; and between 1828 and 1829 (when the government moved subsequently to Nafplion) it was briefly recognised as the capital. It seemed as though history were repeating itself when the first modern Greek coins were minted on Aegina.

The guide to the island has been divided into three sections:
- *Aegina town and Kolona*
- *The north of the island; Palaiochora & Aphaia*
- *The south of the island*

AEGINA TOWN AND KOLONA

AROUND THE HARBOUR

Pausanias points out (*Descrip*. II, 29.2) that the island is 'difficult of approach' because of the sunken rocks and reefs that surround it. There are few harbours and the main port is, and always was, on the upper west coast. The boats from Piraeus skirt the long northern coast and round the low promontory of Cape Plakakia, before turning south to the port. On entering the harbour the extensive ruins of the ancient city (now referred to as 'Kolona', on account of the solitary monolithic column at its centre) are visible on your left. The area where all the boats dock corresponds to the ancient Commercial Harbour, the southern mole of which was rebuilt by Capodistrias on ancient foundations and is an extension of the ancient southern walls of the town. The north mole, forms the

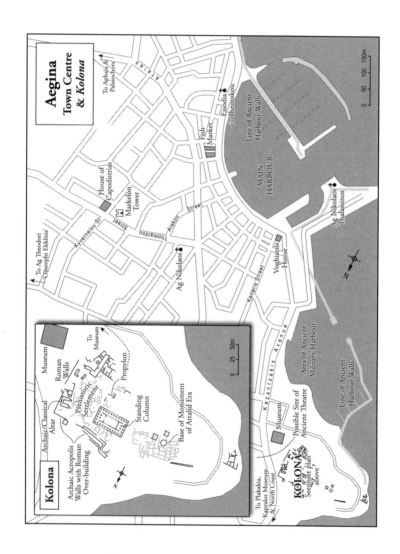

Aegina
Town Centre & Kolona

To Aphaia & Palaeochora

To Ag Theodori 'Omorphi Ekklisia'

Eisodia tis Theotokou

Line of Ancient Harbour Walls

Fish Market

House of Capodistrias

Markelon Tower

To Ag Theodori 'Omorphi Ekklisia'

Kyverneiou St.

Pileos St.

Thomaidou

Aiakou Street

MAIN HARBOUR

Ag Nikolaos

Kanaris Street

Voghiatsis House

Ag Nikolaos Thalassinos

Kazantzakis Avenue

Area of Ancient Military Harbour

Line of Ancient Harbour Walls

0 50 100 150m

Kolona

Museum

Roman Walls

Archaic/Classical Altar

Prehistoric Settlement

Archaic Acropolis Walls with Roman Over-building

To Museum

Propylon

Standing Column

Base of Monument of Attalid Era

Museum

Possible Site of Ancient Theatre

KOLONA
See inset plan above?

To Plakakia, Kapralos Museum & North Coast

0 25 50m

southern boundary of the **ancient Military Harbour** (κρυπτός λιμήν or 'secret harbour'—i.e. of limited access): the remains of its rectangular quays can be seen below the surface of a smooth sea. It is estimated that these could once accommodate as many as 50 triremes.

Towards the seaward end of the mole from the point of disembarkation is the low double-domed church of Aghios Nikolaos Thalassinos, built in a typical vernacular Cycladic style of architecture; in the other direction on the corner by the exit of the port—and in a very different and more international architectural language— is the striking **Voghiatsís Mansion**, a large neoclassical building which dominates the water-front. The Voghiatsís family were prosperous sponge-traders, originally from the island of Symi. The building is a pleasingly proportioned architectural unity, presenting similar but not identical fronts on the two sides of the corner, and with fine wrought-iron balconies supported on marble volutes. Dignified and authoritative, without being overweeningly academic in its neoclassicism, it expresses the best of the spirit of the new statehood of Greece which emerged in the 1820s on this island.

A gracious sweep of buildings, mostly in classicising style, forms the water front, broken towards the southern end by the large Byzantine-style sandstone cathedral church of the *Eisodia tis Theotokou* ('The Presentation of the Virgin'), referred to as the '*Panaghitsa*', built in 1896 and with a marble iconostasis in the interior. In the small palmy square immediately to its north is a bust of Ioannis Capodistrias, first Governor of Independent Greece, who, though a native of Corfu, guided the crucial years of the birth of the Greek State here in Aegina.

IOANNIS CAPODISTRIAS ON AEGINA

When Capodistrias arrived at Aegina on 8 January 1826 it was the first time he had set foot in Aegean Greece. He learned of his appointment as Governor of the new, independent entity of Greece while staying in Geneva where he had retired after his successful negotiation, as envoy of the Russian Tsar, of guarantees for the constitution, independence and neutrality of Switzerland in the aftermath of French dominance and interference under Napoleon. He was, at 51 years of age, a respected and widely experienced politician and international diplomat: a polyglot, a doctor and a person with proven liberal and democratic credentials and charitable instincts. The fractious theatre of nascent Greek politics, dominated by irreconcilable tribal interests and a systemic allergy to sacrifice for the sake of co-operation, was a very different world from the imperial courts of Europe to which he was accustomed. Added to this, he inherited with the job of governing Greece with a virtually empty exchequer. Against this background, he aimed at two objectives: firstly to bring some unity to the Greek military and the country's political class; secondly to begin on wide-ranging reforms of local administration, finance (with the launch of a new coinage), education and public health—the last, a cause to which, as a doctor by training, he was particularly attached. He formalised the borders and the independence of the Greek State in agreement with the international powers. All this was initiated from his modest base in Aegina.

Thoughtful and skilled negotiator though he was, he underestimated the powerful feelings of independence in the rich 'naval islands'—Hydra, Spetses and Psara—which had given so much to the cause of Independence. The first substantial threat to his power came when Hydra resisted a punitive blockade which Capodistrias had planned, by destroying the flagship of the Greek Navy and another of its vessels in the harbour of Poros in August 1831 (see *Battle of Poros*, pp. 108–111). The perpetrator of this act was none other than Andreas Miaoulis from Hydra, the most widely-respected admiral of the Independence War. But Capodistrias's greatest problem was that his world of cosmopolitan diplomacy and high ideals was fundamentally alien to the tribal interests and rebellious egos of local warlords, sharpened by centuries of resistance to Turkish dominion in the mountainous enclaves of the country. In the autumn of 1831, when Capodistrias tried to imprison one of the leaders of the rebels of the Mani, Petrobey Mavromichalis, he was assassinated by Petrobey's brother and son as he went to morning mass in Nauplia.

Aiakou Street, which runs east and perpendicular to the waterfront beside the Port Authority building, leads in (four blocks) towards a small open square dominated by a mediaeval tower, which has something of the look of a Scottish castle imparted to it by the round turrets projecting at the upper corners of the building which still preserve the defensive slits in their under sides. This is the so-called **Márkelon Tower**, a rare survival of the Catalan presence on Aegina in the 14th and 15th centuries:

built with an eye to defence more than comfort, the tower would originally have had fewer windows and a removable staircase or ladder, for access. Opposite the tower across the street is the *Aiginitiko Archontiko* guest-house (*see 'Lodging', below*); this is a typical, small neoclassical house built around a courtyard, with a finely painted ceiling in the main salon upstairs. The whole area uphill from here has many **neoclassical town houses** decorated in pleasing colours and with courtyards bursting with vegetation.

Fifty metres west of the Márkelon Tower is the large modern church of Aghios Nikolaos, built near the site of an Early Christian basilica. An equal distance south east of the tower, on Kyberneion Street, is the house of Capodistrias—which was, in effect, the Government House of the emerging Greek State between 1826 and 1828. (There are two other houses of historic personalities in Aegina: the house of Admiral Constantine Kanaris, who destroyed the core of the Turkish fleet in 1822 (*see under Chios*) in revenge for the massacre of Chios; and the house of Charilaos Trikoupis, Greek statesman and prime minister of the later 19th century. The latter is on the coast road to the south, opposite the cemetery; the former is in Kanaris Street, north of the Voghiatsis Mansion.)

TO THE EAST OF THE CENTRE

Kyverneiou Street is the best point of departure for finding the church of **Aghii Theodori**, which is neither signed nor easy to locate and lies about 2km inland from the port. (*From the house of Capodistrias on Kyverneiou, follow the street uphill (inland) without turning off, until after 1km a busier road crosses at an oblique angle and there is a sandstone church with a red cupola on the right. By continuing here as straight as is possible and taking a narrow concrete road to the right-hand side just beyond the curve on the main road, the church will be on the right after 500m at a junction by an olive tree.*) This tiny 13th century church—in the midst of pistachio orchards—is sometimes simply referred to as the '*Omorphi Ekklisia*', or 'beautiful church'. It appears to be built on the podium of a small ancient building, which stands about 40cm high from the ground, constructed of large rectangular blocks and clearly adapted on its eastern side to accommodate the apse of the church above. The church itself also incorporates a number of ancient blocks, one of which (northwest corner) has a fragmentary Byzantine inscription and what looks like a small part of an architectural drawing below. In the simple interior of the church is an almost complete *cycle of wall-paintings, dating from

1289, which have survived in good condition. In the overall tonality, two iron-oxide pigments—attic yellow and a dark red—predominate to the exclusion of all else. The figures are executed in a vigorous and stylised manner, with much emphasis on the highly-wrought lines of the drapery. A full repertory of scenes from the *Life of Christ* occupy the vault of the church, and a commanding image of the *Virgin and Child flanked by Archangels* occupies the conch of the apse.

TO THE NORTH OF THE CENTRE

The low promontory just to the north of the town is occupied by the archaeological remains of more than five millennia of continuous habitation on the site now referred to as *'**Kolona**'. By the early Bronze Age the settlement here had already grown to be an important centre in prehistoric Greece, and its well-preserved walls and habitations of the 3rd and 2nd millennia BC are amongst the most significant in the Aegean. At the other end of the time line, there are substantial Roman remains and evidence of Byzantine habitation following on thereafter. Excavation began in the late 19th century and continues today, mostly executed by German, Austrian and Greek archaeologists. The site is complex and dense, but a visit first to the **museum** beside the entrance helps to un-pick and make comprehensible the succession of strata on the site. (*Open 8.30–3, closed Mon.*)

The museum

In the first two rooms there are a number of useful reconstructions which give a context to the smaller, fictile objects—in particular the **model of the remarkable two-storey 'White House'**, so-called from the white plaster of its walls: it may well have been inhabited by someone of considerable power and wealth within the community. It dates from c. 2200 BC, but would not look out of place in a Cycladic town today. There are further explanatory models of the development of the fortifications through the 3rd and 2nd millennia, which compare interestingly with those uncovered at Palamari on Skyros. Around the walls in these rooms are the excavated artefacts, beginning with the very early Chalcolithic pieces (c. 3000 BC), including stylised human figurines in a dark-red burnished clay; these are similar to others found across an area stretching from the eastern Peloponnese, through Attica, to Euboea in the east. As the first use of the potter's wheel at the end of the 3rd millennium BC greatly enlarges the possibilities of shape, a variety of design is now found whose clarity and confidence is remarkable: designs which imitate basket-work, abstract forms, and concise **images of ships**, which are revealing of the vigorous maritime commerce and naval power of the island at the time—all dating from before 1800 BC. Many of these show a clear exchange of goods and ideas with Minoan Crete and the Cyclades; indeed some may be the production of workshops supervised by Cretan settlers, such as the massive **storage vase** with perforated handle. Note also the low broad jug with a clear narrative scene showing Odysseus, skillfully depicted clinging to the underbelly of a ram while escaping from the cave of Polyphemus.

The long gallery (*Room 5*) takes the collection into the historical period. In the show case beside the door, the tiny fragment from the back of the head of an early *kouros*, shows the vigorous and un-mechanical working of the stylised hair. The case also contains a stone mould for the serial production of the *aryballos* (a small water container). The centrepiece of the gallery is the lean and alert **sphinx**, a piece of the mid-5th century BC, whose haunches and tail are reminiscent of archaic design, but whose head with fine uncombed hair is notably more Classical in conception. A number of architectural elements, including a finely carved metope, line the walls; some of them preserve vestiges of colour. The final room (*no. 6*) has small fragments from the pedimental sculptures of the Temple of Aphaia—the greater parts of which are in the *Glyptothek* in Munich.

The courtyard displays grave reliefs from the large cemetery on the island of Rheneia, opposite Delos. Outside the museum, along the exterior of its east wall, are shelves of fragments and elements from the site, which are not on display in the museum. There are some fine capitals and architectural elements amongst them, and a notable irregularly shaped altar-top in dark stone with running inscription around its border. Between the museum and the exit is a large fragmentary floor **mosaic of abstract design**, from the **ancient synagogue** of Aegina, dating from the early 4th century AD and showing how—as on Delos—a substantial Jewish community had established itself on Aegina on the strength of the commercial importance which the island still must have possessed at that time. The inscription at its foot commemorates the building and furnishing of the synagogue, with funds provided by the community, during the stewardship of a certain Theodoros and, later, of his son. The synagogue lay inland to the east of the ancient military port.

The site

As you stand in front of the first rise of the site, a basic distinction in building materials is immediately present to view, with the fine (occasionally plastered) archaic construction just above ground level and with the massive rectangular blocks of Classical and Hellenistic work on top of the field of vision; in between is the hastier in-filling with the smaller round stones of re-used prehistoric material. Climbing up, you pass a large, broken storage vase of the classical period *in situ*, and (to the left) vestiges of a clay lined water-tank and drainage-pipe.

Emerging at the top, the **prehistoric structures**, which have followed the rise of the hill, are now revealed to the right (east). The forms of well-heads, mill-stones, doorways, and ovens (under a lean-to roof) are visible, with the occasional parts of Archaic and Classical structures, at a higher level, above them. The site has good explanatory displays which are necessary for making sense of a complex superimposition of many layers—10 different levels in the prehistoric settlement alone, going back to the first human evidence of the 5th millennium BC. By about 2500 BC we find substantial dwellings whose external flights of steps suggests they possessed a second floor; by 2200 BC, there emerge the first clear fortifications. At this point development was interrupted by a conflagration in c. 2050 BC; but the town soon rose again with greater strength and renewed commercial activity indicated by the presence of Minoan and Cycladic pottery; the fortifications were extended towards the east. The burial place of a hero-warrior dating from the 17th century BC lies about 20m to the south east: when excavated it was found to contain finely crafted weapons, a helmet and gold diadem. Then, in common with all the Mycenaean sites on the mainland, there is a clear break in habitation in 1200 BC.

Behind, to the west, are the remains of the Classical **Temple of Apollo**, which stood on a high platform and dominated the skyline. This is the third such temple on the site, and dates from c. 510 BC: the first was erected in around 600 BC, and the second, which appears to have been destroyed by fire, was built a half-century later. The last temple, to whose *opisthodomos* (the rear chamber behind the naos) the one standing column belonged, was a conventional Doric temple, facing east, with 6 x 11 monolithic columns in its peristyle. The path crosses the stone platform which surrounded the temple's high podium: the platform is carefully crafted, with a fine upper edge to the stone and an irregular rustication of the vertical face. It is interesting that there is no overall organised plan of the exact size of the blocks: the construction appears to proceed by rule of thumb. A section of the *temenos* wall of the sanctuary is conserved just to the north; and the temple's large altar can be seen some distance to the east.

From the northeast corner of the temple-platform can been seen the superimposition of **fortifications of different epochs**. In the vertical wall facing, the rougher stonework of the prehistoric (middle Bronze Age) walls below is surmounted by later Hellenistic fortifications in regular blocks—themselves re-used pieces from Archaic construction, some of which have the letters of inscriptions in their surface. To the left, the late Antique rectangular tower is built over a bastion of the prehistoric walls. But the imposing magnitude of the fortifications can only be appreciated by descending from the north side of the temple and going outside the walls. Towards the eastern end, it is possible to see three periods together: the irregular stones of the prehistoric walls set back behind the clean lines of the Archaic fortifications added in front, with Roman additions standing even further out from the city. The view of the ramparts from here is impressive and gives a clear sense of the compact unity which a settlement of this period presented to the outside world.

To the west of the temple of Apollo, the city extends in a tight-knit web of prehistoric houses. Only the bases of two or three later Hellenistic constructions are clearly visible above them: these date from the period of Pergamon's possession of Aegina, and one may represent the remains of a monument to the Attalid dynasty.

The coast road beyond Kolona continues due north, passing a number of large villas with gardens—the four-

square form of the Zaimis Tower and the more traditional Venizelos House in a secluded garden of dense palms.
At the point of Cape Plakakia, with its historic lighthouse
built in 1881, the road begins to run east and after 1km
passes, on the left, a large bronze statue of a barefooted
slightly stooped woman in traditional dress: this is a work
entitled *My Mother*—one of a series of sensitive studies
of his mother, by the artist, Christos Kapralós. Opposite,
across the road, is the **Kapralós Museum**. (*Open June–Oct,
daily except Mon 10–2, 6–8; Nov–May Fri, Sat, Sun 10–2*)

The small collection here presents an overview of the work
of Kapralós, both as sculptor and painter. He worked during the summers of the last 30 years of his life in this house,
from 1963 until his death in 1993. There is considerable variety of styles and mediums in his work. The free-standing
sculptures on show here are mostly in a polished eucalyptus
wood, and are much influenced by early Cycladic sculpture
forms, although the artist's priority was to allow the natural
shape and patterns of the wood itself to suggest and direct
the creation. The pieces are often characterised by dramatic
pose and tension. His narrative works owe more to Classical influences: the last room in the museum exhibits a cast
of Kapralós's epic work, completed in 1956, celebrating the
Battle of Pindus. It is a long continuous frieze in low-relief—

somewhat static in conception—which tells the story of
Greece's history since independence, the original of which,
in local *poros* stone, is now displayed in one of the halls of
the Parliament building in Athens. The artist's paintings,
predominantly of nude figures, which are on exhibition
here clearly show how his natural medium of expression
was through the volumes and tactile appeal of sculpture. In
1962, Kapralós represented Greece at the Venice *Biennale*.

Two hundred metres further east along the coast road,
on the point of the peninsula, is a low, somewhat severe
building where Nikos Kazantzakis wrote *The Life and
Times of Alexis Zorba.*

The next, small promontory to the east, after a further
300m, is a flat apron of land jutting into the bay towards
the north. It is the site of an ancient quarry of *poros* stone,
which had easy access for shipping by barge. At the sea
front, the cuts in the bed-rock are shallow but clear, reminiscent of Pouriá in Skyros: further south however (i.e.
closer to the road), the deeper cuts are not those of a
quarry but the rectangular *loculi* of an ancient necropolis.
It would seem that the quarry came first and, at a later
date—perhaps as late as the 1st century AD—it was adapted to become a burial ground.

THE NORTH OF THE ISLAND

The north of the island is best explored by taking the road that heads east from the southern extremity of the waterfront, Phaneromenis Street. This is the main road to Aghios Nektarios and the Temple of Aphaia. The road passes, to the right, the former **Orphanage** built by Capodistrias for the children orphaned by the War of Independence—subsequently converted into a prison and now standing empty. A further 500m down the road, is the ruined church of the **Panaghia Phaneromeni**—a large 18th century basilica-church, characterised by its wide, round-arched doors and windows, which are pleasingly framed in marble on the west front. There is a crypt below the church.

To the east of the town, the road soon climbs into the varied and beautiful landscape of the centre of the island. The sparse foliage of the immaculate **orchards of pistachio** and olive trees against the pale terracotta-coloured earth beneath creates an effect characteristic of Aegina's landscape: and the mature Aleppo pine-trees which form the dark backdrop to it all, complete what is a striking combination of colours and textures.

THE PISTACHIO OF AEGINA

The angular and sparse growth of the pistachio tree gives it an appearance similar to the fig-tree; but its glossy and smaller foliage is quite different. The fruit forms in abundant clusters of lupin-shaped capsules which, although a yellowy green at first, soon acquire a beautiful pale red tinge which enlivens the whole tree: these are the forming nuts. They have adapted easily to the soil and very mild climate of Aegina, and have become its most famous product. They have a rounder form than other pistachio nuts. The pistachio tree is native to the hot dry climate of an area that stretches from southeastern Turkey to eastern Iran, but in the mild climate and clayey soil of Aegina it appears also to have found a congenial home. The progenitors of the *pistacio vera* trees on Aegina were first brought here from Syria in 1860.

Four kilometres from Aegina is the road junction at Kondos, with the huge pilgrimage church of **Aghios Nektarios** dominating the view to the north. The traveller, intent on the antiquities of Aphaia and the Byzantine churches of Palaiochora, may be tempted to pass by this piece of modernity; but a visit here is instructive and not

without considerable reward. The main building, which
is actually dedicated to the Aghia Triada (Holy Trinity),
must be the largest church to be built in Greece in the
last 100 years. Its octagonal form and shallow cupola are
deliberately Constantinopolitan in design, and the mass
of coloured marbles inside and carved, 'basket' capitals
are surely a deliberate imitation of Justinian's Haghia
Sophia. The **apsidal mosaic** of the Virgin and Christ and
the Archangels Michael and Gabriel, with all the islands
of the Saronic Gulf laid out below their feet, is a work
of surprising beauty. The church was begun in 1973, and
the mosaic finished in 1999. The pre-existing monastery
above, reached via a serpentine ramp, contains a highly
decorated chapel enshrining the grave of Aghios Nektarios, who died in 1920 and was canonised in 1961.

Almost opposite the entrance to the complex of Aghios
Nektarios and a few metres to the west is a road which
leads south across the valley and up the hillside opposite,
to the isolated monastery of the **Panaghia** or **Theotókos
Chrysoleóntissa** (3km). This is everything that Aghios
Nektarios is not—remote, old and peaceful, in a wild valley of the interior where there is little sound beyond the
wailing of peacocks and bleating of goats. The foundation of the monastery is much older than the buidlings:
it was originally situated by the coast at Leonti, just west

of Vathí in the north of the island and was moved, together with its holy icons, to this isolated site for greater
protection in the first decade of the 17th century. The
fine pre-existing 15th century machicolated tower at the
centre of the monastery complex provided a focus and a
safe treasury around which the monastery could be constructed. Although founded as a male community, it became a nunnery in 1935 and currently has eleven resident
nuns. The original *catholicon* burnt down and the present
one dates from the late 17th century. The heavily carved
wooden **iconostasis** is from 1670: much of it has been
over-varnished, but its doors have escaped this treatment
and possess fine, polychrome figures of Christ and St Peter with keys.

PALAIOCHORA

The northward branch of the road at Kondos/Aghios
Nektarios leads after 1km to the site of ***Palaiochora**, the
Byzantine capital of the island for nearly 1,000 years between the 9th and 19th centuries. Now deserted, all that is
left is its multitude of churches scattered over the barren
hillside, robbed of the dense urban context that once en-
folded them on all sides. Comparable with Palaiochora on
Kythera, and Kastro on Skiathos, many of these and other

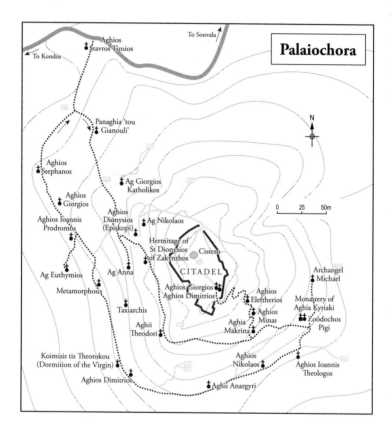

Palaiochora

To Souvala

To Kondòs

Aghios
stavros Timios

Panaghia 'tou
Gianoúli'

Aghios
Stephanos

Ag Giorgios
Katholikos

Aghios
Giorgios

Aghios
Dionysios
(Episkopi)

Ag Nikolaos

Aghios Ioannis
Prodromos

Hermitage of
St Dionysios
of Zakynthos

Cistern

CITADEL

Ag Euthymios

Ag Anna

Metamorphosis

Taxiarchis

Aghios Giorgios
Aghios Dimitrios

Archangel
Michael

Aghios
Eleftherios

Monastery of
Aghia Kyriaki

Aghii
Theodori

Aghios
Minas

Zoödochos
Pigi

Aghia
Makrina

Koimisis tis Theotokou
(Dormition of the Virgin)

Aghios
Nikolaos

Aghios Dimitrios

Aghios Ioannis
Theologos

Aghii Anargyri

N

0   25   50m

similar Byzantine sites were first chosen and inhabited in the 9th century when Saracen Arab raids forced the inhabitants of the settlements of Antiquity to abandon and seek new and fortifiable refuges inland which would be inaccessible to raiders. This did not, however, protect the site here from the destructive attentions of Khaireddin Barbarossa in 1537 and of further pillaging when the city was re-taken by the Venetians under Morosini in 1654. Palaiochora itself was only abandoned after the safety of coastal habitation had become vouchsafed once again in the last two centuries. Although habitation dwindled during the Turkish occupation of the 18th century, in the 1820s there were still a good 400 habitations on this site: the speed with which they have all disappeared is remarkable. (*A visit to the site involves a pleasant ramble around the hill. In theory, most of the churches are open all the time, and the guardian at the Episkopi church will open any that happen to be closed on request: but there are no hard-and-fast rules or times for his presence. Patience may be required by the dedicated Byzantinist who wishes to see everything inside and out. The following itinerary covers the site in roughly clockwise fashion, climbing to the left after entering.*)

The Churches of Palaiochora

Below the road to the left as you arrive is the 16th century church of Aghios Charalambos, with a double nave—a common plan for several churches on this site. The path into the main part of the site begins beside the 15th century church of the **Aghios Stavros Timios** ('The Holy Venerable Cross') beside the road. The church is still in current use for liturgies, and has wall-paintings along its the north wall, which have been retouched, probably in the 19th century. The small scene of the bound and entombed Christ in the north niche of the *prothesis*, behind the *templon* screen, has an unexpected pathos: it is probably contemporary with the building of the church. The path to the left, passing the ruined church of the 'Panaghia tou Gianouli' (with carved Byzantine eagle on one of the supporting pillars) leads up to the important church of **Aghios Giorgios Katholikos**, which stood on the only square in the settlement, the so-called '*foro*' (marketplace). The church contains a dramatic and beautiful, early 15th century painting in the apse of the *Virgin and Child*, both with extended arms and hands in blessing. An inscription over the door bears the date of a Venetian restoration of the church in 1533. The design of the interior is odd, and it represents a plan peculiar to this settlement—in which the long axis of the church is oriented transversely, and the sanctuary, with iconostasis and apse, is located (in this case) in the far northeastern corner, while the entrance to the church is in the southwestern corner. Although a little disorienting, this may simply be due to a need to have the space for a larger congregation in a church where the steep slope of the site did not permit any further extension along the normal longitudinal axis. There were once relics of St George in this church, but they were sold by the inhabitants to the Venetians in the 16th century and are now kept in the church of San Giorgio Maggiore in Venice.

A small white marble fragment is immured in the exterior wall of Aghios Giorgios Katholikos; in fact, there are marble columns, lintels and capitals scattered all around the area—some Byzantine, some ancient, indicating that the site may well also have seen an earlier, ancient presence. The 15th century church of **Aghios Dionysios**, called the **'Episkopi' church**, a little higher up, is the principal church of the settlement. There are fine Byzantine Imperial eagles and a cross above the door, the whole of which was once brightly coloured. To its right, as you enter, are two carved stone steps leading to a stone seat or platform: this is an interesting detail, possibly the base of a marble canopy for the display of icons on feast days, or else a throne used on particular occasions by the bishop in the period when the area in front of the church was a completely covered portico. The domed interior has an aisle to the left which was added nearly 200 years later during the renovations of 1610 which are referred to in a painted inscription. The church can be seen in model-form, held by SS. Peter and Paul, in the paintings on the south wall—an unusual state of affairs, since such models are usually held by the saint to whom the church is dedicated, in this case St Dionysios. These paintings are the work of one Demetrios of Athens, according to the inscription. The small church of Aghios Nikolaos, with carved lintel, is just above and to the east.

Continuing from the church of the Episkopi, you pass the tiny hermitage of St Dionysios of Zakynthos to the right, with the church of St Anne below, and further along the ridge, the church of the **Aghii Theodori**: this has a number of wall-paintings, the best preserved being the *Crucifixion* scene on the west wall and the saints over the door arch. The path turns east and, climbing past a cluster of three churches, Aghii Makrina, Minas and Eleftherios, reaches the remains of the **citadel** on the summit, built in 1462 by the Venetians during their first occupation of the site. It is interesting how hidden the whole site is from the sea, and yet what excellent views it commands of every approach from this vantage point. The walls are best preserved in the northeast sector. On the summit, however, only the remains of two cisterns and the foundations of magazines are visible, apart from the twin churches of Aghios Giorgios and Aghios Demetrios—

the two soldier saints whom one might have expected to find honoured in the keep of a castle. The parallel and inter-communicating design of the two churches, which were built in the late 17th century, may have facilitated the celebration of both the Greek and Latin rite at the time of the Venetian occupation.

Descending once again by the same path, past Aghia Makrina, will bring you to a corner of the site which gives some sense of the intimate and pleasingly irregular spaces of a Byzantine town: this is the **monastery of Aghia Kyriaki**, with the ruined remains of its monastic buildings around it. In effect, it is a double church, because it has a parallel nave to the north of comparable size dedicated to the **Zoödochos Pigi** (the Virgin as the 'Fount of Life'): this has interesting wall-paintings from the 17th century, amongst which is a fine *Second Coming of Christ*. The last church, beyond the monastery at the end of the path, is the church of the **Archangel Michael**: on the exterior, around the arch above the door in its south wall, are some beautiful decorative details—a couple of them seem almost Celtic in inspiration.

Taking the lower path back westwards towards the entrance, you pass a number of churches with decorative interest. **Aghios Ioannis Theologos**, with 14th century paintings (in poor condition) in the apse, cupola and walls of the nave; perhaps best preserved is the St George on the south wall by the door. Outside the door is part of a finely carved early Byzantine column with palm motif.

Aghios Nikolaos, a little further to the west, confronts the visitor on entering the church with the large depiction of *Four Saints* in ivory-coloured tunics (15th century), painted almost in monochrome. The church has the lateral-axis design observed already in Aghios Giorgios Katholikos, which makes the confrontation with the four martyrs even more dramatic. The other wall paintings have been re-touched in the course of the 19th century.

Further west again lies the church of the **Aghii Anargyri**, with (largely fragmentary) paintings of considerable interest. Around the west door is a fine *Christ in Majesty*, and on the south wall (by the west door) an uncommon depiction of *Abraham in Paradise*. The greatest delight lies in a tiny fragment above, which shows a ship at sea beside a mountainous island: the boat is sustained by 'Saintly Piety', while capricious winds blow through their trumpets to either side and the ocean pullulates with octopi, sea-serpents, crabs, and many-headed monsters, below the terrified mariners. Note also the Antique column fragment with small Ionic capital embedded in the south wall.

After the churches of Aghios Dimitrios, and of the Koimisis tis Theotokou (Dormition of the Virgin), whose paintings have unfortunately suffered whitewashing and over-painting in the 20th century, the path, turning north again, comes to the early 14th century church of the **Metamorphosis**, or Transfiguration, which has paintings—perhaps contemporary with the building—in the sanctuary and apse. Above the *Virgin and Child* in the apse, there is a scene of the Old Testament *Trinity of angels seated at the table of Sarah and Abraham*: this sets a theme for many of the other New Testament 'table' scenes nearby—most notably, and best preserved of all, the *Last Supper* on the right side. Almost directly up the steep slope from the Metamorphosis is the domed church of the Taxiarchis (*currently closed for restoration*): this has 14th century wall-paintings inside and an antique column incorporated into the *templon*.

The other churches on this slope have paintings that are less well-preserved. Those in Aghios Ioannis Prodromos (below the path) are possibly of the early 13th century, but have been partially repainted in recent times. The church of Aghios Euthymios (further below) has later murals of the 16th century, showing *SS. Constantine and Helen with the True Cross*. Many of the churches on this slope have widely varying orientations, ranging from northeast (Aghios Euthymios) to almost due south (the Koimisis tis Theotokou and the Metamorphosis): this is often dictated by the lie of the land and the space available. The two remaining churches are no exception to this: just above the path, the church of **Aghios Giorgios** is oriented to the south: on its nave wall (here on the west side) is an interesting representation of the *Prophet Elijah*, with the raven and its gift of bread. Across the path and below is another lateral-axis church, Aghios Stephanos, with a boxed apse in the northeast corner.

The road beyond Palaiochora to the north winds rapidly down to the sea offering wide views across the water to Athens and the Attic peninsula. It joins the coast near to the attractive harbour of **Souvala** (which has summer connections with Piraeus). In the bay, 1km east of the village, there are **radioactive springs** (*the Thermal Station on the shore is currently closed*). From here it is a pleasant drive eastwards along the coast to the small port of Vaghía, where the road turns inland and rejoins the central route of the island just before it climbs the pine-clad hill up to Aphaia.

APHAIA

The ***Temple of Aphaia** is one of the most important and beautiful in Greece. Its site on a panoramic hill-top at the northeastern point of the island is magnificent, and its state of preservation (though reconstructed in certain areas) is excellent. It is a relatively early temple (late sixth

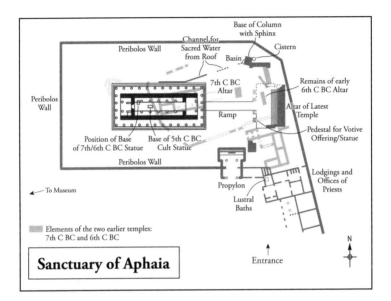

Base of Column
with Sphinx

Channel for
Sacred Water
from Roof

Cistern

Peribolos Wall

Basin

7th C BC
Altar

Remains of early
6th C BC Altar

Peribolos
Wall

Altar of Latest
Temple

Ramp

Pedestal for Votive
Offering/Statue

Position of Base
of 7th/6th C BC Statue

Base of 5th C BC
Cult Statue

Peribolos Wall

Lodgings and
Offices of
Priests

To Museum

Propylon

Lustral
Baths

Elements of the two earlier temples:
7th C BC and 6th C BC

Entrance

N

Sanctuary of Aphaia

century BC); it once displayed magnificent sculptural decorations which still exist (in Munich and Athens); and it
still possesses many of the elements of an Ancient sanctuary which have generally been lost at other sites. Early
in the day, it is a tranquil site, and there are few places in
Greece where the feel and the entirety of a place of ancient cult can be better sensed. (*Open 8.30–3.30, closed
Mon.*)

The dedication to 'Aphaia'

There are no other temples dedicated to Aphaia and there
is some uncertainty about who or what the name refers
to. An important inscription (now in the museum on the
site) found in 1901 and dating from the mid 6th century
BC gives the dedication, while stating that: 'When Theoitas
was priest, the dwelling/temple was made for Aphaia, and
the altar and the ivory were added, and the [?throne] was
completed'. The name 'Aphaia' appears to be cognate with
φαίνειν, 'to make clear' or 'appear', modified by the negative
prefix 'α-'. Whoever Aphaia was, it seems she 'did not appear'.
Tradition, passed through later writers, links her with the
Cretan goddess Britomartis who may have been honoured
here under the local name, manifestation or epithet, 'Aphaia'.
This link is consonant with the Minoan Cretan trading presence clearly evident at Kolona (*see above*). Britomartis was

a daughter of Zeus (note that Mount Oros, with its sanctuary sacred to Zeus Hellanios is directly visible from here), and she was therefore half-sister to Artemis, to whom her cult seems to be related and with whom she shared a love of hunting, solitude and chastity. It may have happened that, in fleeing from the unwanted sexual attentions of King Minos of Crete, Britomartis was made invisible ('ἀφἄνής') by Artemis and transported to the safety of Aegina. Artemis herself is also associated with the moon, which has phases of invisibility, and this may be a further element in the complex composition of Aphaia's identity. Pindar is known to have composed a hymn in Aphaia's honour, but its loss deprives of us of much valuable information. We can only guess at what Aphaia's particular sphere of influence or protection might have been, though the nurturing of children appears to have been an important part of it: her temple, however, would have been a place principally of female cult.

Previous temples on the site

Traces of human presence on this site go as far back as c. 3000 BC, and a sanctuary appears to have been created in the Late Bronze Age. Indeed the cult of Aphaia may have been current already for over a millennium at the time the first stone temple was erected here. In historic times, however, the existing temple is the second or third such temple on the site. An altar is visible which belonged to a first temple that predates 570 BC. Of the second temple, which immediately precedes the present one, substantial foundations can still be seen: this temple was begun in 570 BC and is the one to which the Theoitas inscription, cited above, belonged. It burned down in around 510 BC and its sculptural fragments were, as was customary, buried in the earth movements necessary to prepare the platform of the new (third) temple, which was probably begun almost immediately after and completed shortly after 490 BC.

Layout of the sanctuary

Clearly visible at Aphaia (*see plan*) are many of the constituent elements of a temple complex which have tended to be obliterated in other sanctuaries: the foundations of the *peribolos* or perimeter-wall all round the temple, defining the sacred area; the *propylaia*, or monumental gateway, through which the suppliants entered; the dwellings on the edge of the area for the priests and the ritual baths they would have used. The form of the altar to the east is well conserved, too, with the bases for dedicatory sculptures in front of it. A ramp here (not a particularly common element in sanctuaries) joins the altar to the east entrance of the temple. Finally, in the northeast corner, a visible channel in the temple platform leads the (sacred) rain-water from the roof to a cistern below. Together with the good state of conservation of the temple-structure itself and the setting which has been little altered through the centuries, this provides a uniquely complete picture of a Greek sanctuary of the Archaic and Classical eras.

Colour

Brilliant strong colour was an important feature of Archaic and early Classical sculpture and architecture. Later, as taste changed, the polychrome may have become less vibrant and less universal in later Antiquity. Not only were pedimental sculptures coloured and set against a coloured background to make them more life-like and easier to read from a distance, but the architectural elements of the area of the architrave and above were emphasised and picked out chromatically. In a case such as this temple, which is constructed out of a poor-quality local *poros* stone, by comparison with the fine Pentelic marble of the Parthenon across the bay, a layer of stucco plaster was applied to the columns and lower elements of the building. This was a common feature of Greek temples in Sicily, where there was poorer building stone and where vestiges of the stucco (esp. at Selinunte) still remain. The stucco gave the building a white colour very different from the more tender honey-colour of its bare stone which is visible today. Whether this stucco was a bright, intense white, or whether it was modified to become an ivory colour is hard to determine with certainty.

Pediment sculptures

The history of the sculptural decoration is complicated by the fact that the first two series for the pediments of the existing temple, produced between 510 and 500 BC, were removed after what was less than a decade and replaced by two newer series, executed in c. 500 BC (west pediment) and c. 490 BC (east pediment). Were all of these ensembles still complete, they would provide one of the most revealing studies in the development of Greek sculpture at what is, in effect, the most important moment of transition in its long history. The reasons for this surprising replacement of the pediment may have a political origin: this was after all the period of Aegina's greatest power and its bitterest confrontation with Athens. The first pediment sculptures commissioned for the new temple portrayed stories from Aegina's legendary past: the fight of Telamon (son of Aiacus of Aegina) and Hercules against the Amazons in the presence of Athena (west pediment); and the abduction of the nymph Aegina by Zeus (east pediment). At the time it was decided to change this programme the east pediment was already in place, while the west pediment may possibly not yet have been fully completed and positioned. These were

then removed and set up on display in the precinct in front
of the east façade of the temple, since they remained the
property of the goddess. New sculpture groups were then
commissioned of the same workshop, probably under the
same master. This time they were to show scenes, again in
the presiding presence of Athena, of Aeginetan heroes during the campaigns against Troy: the west pediment showed
the participation, in the siege of Troy, of Ajax—son of Telamon, protégé of Hercules, and descendant of Aiacus and of
Zeus—who was much honoured in Aegina; the east pediment showed a scene from an earlier Trojan campaign in
which Aiacus himself—son of Zeus by Aegina—together
with Hercules, stormed Troy and killed the king and all his
sons, except one, the future King Priam. It appears that, at
the climax of their struggles with Athens around 500 BC the
Aeginetans wished to emphasise the heroic prowess of their
forefathers in battles with an earlier enemy, Troy, over the
blander legendary scenes which figured in the earlier pediments. The change is very revealing: but yet more fascinating
is a subtle change in style between the two new pediments
which substituted the old ones—the new west pediment of
c. 500 BC and the new east pediment of ten years later. The
first is a beautifully patterned arrangement of discrete elements and figures with the stylised faces and poses of high
Archaic narrative art; the second is an integrated drama of

related, more humanised figures, with softer lineaments. The pediment has ceased to be just a patterned design and is becoming a living stage for human drama in the last of the pediment groups.

Although fragments of these pediments are exhibited in the museum at Kolona, and in the National Archaeological Museum in Athens, the great majority of the sculptures are in the Munich *Glyptothek*. They were first excavated on the site by Carl von Hallerstein and Charles Robert Cockerell in 1811: they were shipped via Athens, Zakynthos and Malta, to Rome, where they were purchased by Ludwig I of Bavaria. They were restored, arranged and completed according to a design by Thorvaldsen. Between 1962 and 1971, this (by now, much criticised) method of display was dismantled, all the additions removed, and a systematic and academic attempt was made to exhibit only the original fragments in their most probable original arrangement. This is how they are seen today. The sculptures are executed in marble from the island of Paros.

On approaching the temple from the entrance below, it is important always to recall the fact that there are the remains of two stone temples on this site, that the present one is the temple of 510 BC and that, at a slightly lower level, there are vestiges of the older preceding temple of

570 BC visible at many points. The latter was perhaps only a quarter of the size of the existing temple, had a much smaller sanctuary area and was—for what reason we cannot be sure—oriented very slightly differently from the newer temple: its remains therefore are always going to be at an oblique angle to everything later. The early temple was oriented probably 20–25° north of a true east/west axis, while the later one was only c.10° north of the true axis.

To the left, as you climb up towards the terrace, the ashlar-masonry base of the perimeter wall, or *peribolos*, of the existing temple-sanctuary is visible. This would have been higher and finished with an upper section in mud-brick. To the right are the **foundations of the *propylaia***, or monumental gate of entrance. Visible is the stump of one of its interior octagonal columns. This roofed gateway would have provided a moment of shade before emerging into the dazzling light of the temple's sanctuary and would have framed a partial—and beautiful—view of the temple. Further to the right, beyond this area, are visible the plastered **lustral basins** used for ritual ablutions by those officiating. Yet further over to the right are the foundations of a series of rooms which constituted the quarters of the priests and the administrators of the sanctuary.

The upper **terrace** where the temple stands is artificially constructed; its consolidation would have been effected by burying the remains of the earlier burnt temple and flattening the top with dressed stone. Much of the stone for building both temples will, in turn, have come from substantial cutting of the irregular top of the hill in order to flatten it into a terrace: this excess stone will have been cut into architectural elements, which will have been further supplemented by stone quarried just below the site. A deep cut in the terrace in front of the south side of the temple reveals a piece of the perimeter-wall of the earlier temple sanctuary.

The south face of the temple shows immediately the **degree of conservation** of the architectural detail on the temple. The perfectly clear fluting of the tapering columns, the minimal concentric decoration on the Doric capitals, the triglyphs (once painted dark blue, with their vertical grooves defined in black), the clear, hanging *guttae* below—all the variety of architectural elements which derive from an earlier age when temples were constructed, doweled and pegged out of wooden elements, and which the Greeks meticulously preserved when they began to construct in stone—are seen more clearly here than in many other temples. Grooves are visible in the sides of the triglyphs, into which the decorated metopes were slotted:

given the width of the groove it seems likely that these were either made of wood or of terracotta. None has survived.

The area to the east of the temple is extraordinarily complete in what it shows us of the working of the sanctuary. A clearly defined **ramp** runs axially between the east (front) door of the temple and the altar whose base is visible 25m east of the temple, almost at the edge of the sanctuary. The **altar** was a large, wide, stepped structure, running parallel to the east front of the temple, preceded by a paved rectangular area: the officiating priest would have faced the rising sun. Two square bases, in front of the paved area and to the south, were the bases for dedicatory statues, and would have been balanced by two others to the north.

Two earlier altars are also visible: the roped-off area to the north of the paved way between the altar and temple is the base of the altar belonging to the first temple of around 600 BC; back nearer to the altar, the stone areas running at an obtuse angle to the temple axis and at a lower level, are the base of the altar of the second temple of 570 BC. All the foundations, oriented on the same axis, to the south date from this second temple: these were the administrative buildings for the sanctuary and its entrance gate. Also of the same period are the square pedestal and water cistern on the northern edge of the terrace. On the **pedestal** stood a 14m column crowned by a sculpted sphinx—the only monument to stand in the same place during the lifetime of both temples. The **cistern** collected the rainwater from the roof and the stylobate of the temple; a small **channel** (still visible) paved in the floor of the sanctuary terrace led from the temple down to a shallow basin and thence into the cistern. The water which fell on the temple had a sacred quality and could be collected in this manner to be used for ritual purposes. Further along the northern side, a deep cut in the terrace reveals the perimeter wall of the much smaller area of the sanctuary belonging to the earlier temple of 570 BC.

The superstructure of the building has been reconstructed at various points and this is most visible at the **western end**, where the sharp-cut, smoother stone is modern and clearly distinguishable from the original material. The view inside from the western end is revealing of the construction of the building and of many of the classic 'optical corrections' used in temple construction. The slight rise towards the centre of the stylobate is visible; and the increased diameter of the corner columns, so as to give the impression of greater strength at the corners, is also perceptible. From here it can be seen that the architrave consists of two parallel blocks set side by side; and that the support of the roof of the *naos*, was on a double colonnade, with the *entasis* or tapering of the columns following through from the lower columns into the form of the upper ones. The exposed ends of the architrave of the lower colonnade in the interior, display U-shaped grooves cut into the perpendicular face of each piece: around these a rope could be run for lifting the blocks into place. This can be seen also on a number of pieces lying on the ground in the vicinity.

The interior of the temple once contained two cult statues of Aphaia; one small, older image in wood with an ivory surface, which belonged to the earlier temple and was placed in the northwestern corner of the *naos* on a stone base which is still visible; the second, more than life-size, statue was made together with the construction of the existing temple around 505 BC (a fragment of its acrolithic arm is in the National Archaeological Museum in Athens). Its place was in the centre of the shrine; the holes for the posts which held a wooden barrier surrounding it can still be seen in the floor of the *naos*.

Museum (40m downhill of the west side of the temple)
The three rooms of the tiny museum on the site are well labelled and explained. There are two floors: the upper

(ground) floor relates to the existing temple, the lower floor to the previous 6th century BC building. The first room, at entrance level, contains some building remains, reconstruction models and fragments with helpful reconstructions of the positioning of elements of sculptures in the pediments. There are marble pan-tiles and covers from the perimeter of the roof (the body of which was in terracotta tiles). The small collection's most important exhibits are on the floor below, where some fragments of the triglyph/metope succession of the entablature still retain their brilliant and astonishing colouring in (Egyptian) blue, (iron oxide) red, (bistre) black and (malachite) green. The inscription mentioning the name of Aphaia can also be seen here, as well as a model and a partial reconstruction of the pediment and entablature of the 6th century temple, which was of a tetra-style *in antis* design.

In spite of being a roofless skeleton today, the temple is a relic of great presence. Its decoration and colour, and the play of light and shade which would have been created by the roof and the eaves, are all gone. Nonetheless, the counterpoint of clear forms—rectangles, diagonals and cylinders—still gives immense satisfaction when seen against the backdrop of the sky and of the dark, irregular volumes of the Aleppo pines. Sadly, we cannot know what trees covered the surrounding hill in Antiquity—if any.

Beyond Aphaia the road descends steeply to the coastal resort of Aghia Marina, grouped attractively around a small port amidst dense pine trees. There are direct connections with Piraeus from here during the summer period.

THE SOUTH OF THE ISLAND

Two roads leave Aegina for the south of the island: one follows the coast, the other heads southeast on a plateau which crosses the centre of the island to the south. This latter rises quite sharply outside the town and offers wide views of the coast and of the sea towards Angistri and the Peloponnese. After 6.5km it passes the hamlet of **Pachia Rachi**, built as the name implies along a spur of the hill ('*rachi*' means a crest or ridge)—a charming and peaceful village of stone buildings, spread around the colourful bell tower of its church. Immediately beyond the village to the east is the *Hellenic Centre and Clinic for Wild Animals*, dedicated to the care of stranded or wounded wild animals which are reintegrated into the wild, where possible, after cure and treatment. Less than 1km further

down the road, a track signposted to the church of the
Taxiarchis leads to the right towards the slopes of Mount
Oros which dominates the landscape at this point. The
small church with its red roof and octagonal drum is visible from afar, now totally isolated in the barren and rocky
hillside, but once the centre of a monastic community. It
is only as one begins to get nearer that the massive ashlar-masonry retaining walls on which its stands, come into
view.

The terraces created by these impressive walls, and the
monumental flight of steps which separates them, are
what remains of the sanctuary and **Temple of Zeus *Hellanios***, 'Zeus, giver of rain'—a cult which was brought to
the island by Dorian settlers around 1000 BC. The scale
of the construction here and its imposing strength have
a calculated appropriateness to the mightiest of the Olympian gods. What is visible today is the last phase of
the site's development—mostly Hellenistic construction
of impressively dressed and cut stone (in particular on
the left of the flight of steps), which dates from the 3rd
century BC when, during the Pergamene domination of
the island, the whole mountain was held sacred. A place
of cult had already been here for a long time before, however.

The 7m wide, **processional staircase** gives the site an

unexpected monumentality. The building material here came from the cutting away of the hillside when the terraces were first levelled, and it may have been during that process that the springs behind the sanctuary were opened up. Today there is little more than a black Stygian rock-cut hole with standing water in it, just above the site; but the presence of neatly cut conduit channels for flowing water, along both the south and east sides of the terrace under and against the hill, suggests that the water here was once far from stagnant. Nothing remains of the temple which was here, and which a combination of earthquakes and early Christian zeal has deleted. But the massive quantity of rubble would suggest that the buildings were of imposing size. Many of these large, regularly-cut blocks have been incorporated into the **church of the Taxiarchis**, which sits on the northwest corner of the temple's *crepis*. The present church appears to be a 13th century structure, although it probably replaces an earlier foundation on the same site. The contemporaneous **wall-paintings** in its interior are impressive, though damaged. Again, the iron-oxide reds and yellows predominate, as observed at the *Omorphi Ekklesia* on the edge of Chora: here, however, there is greater sophistication in the painting of the magnificently detailed armour of the *Archangel Michael*, and of an unusual and graceful scene depicting the dream of *Jacob's Ladder* with angels flowing between Paradise and Earth, in the southwest segment of the drum of the dome.

Mount Oros, known as *Panhellenion* to the ancients, dominates the scene from behind. The barren, rocky mountain (531m) has a pure shape which was a conspicuous landmark for mariners in the Saronic Gulf. The gathering of clouds on its peak is said to be a sure sign of rain, a phenomenon noted in Antiquity. Legend also relates how Aiacus, the mythical early king of Aegina, successfully interceded with Zeus, on the advice of the Delphic Oracle, to bring rain to end a drought which had afflicted the island for many years. The summit is reached in 50 minutes by a path from the saddle on the western side of the mountain. At several points and levels just beneath the summit, to west and to east, there are outcrops of ancient wall which belong to a Mycenaean sanctuary of the 13th century BC. To the north of the chapel (dedicated to the *Analipsi*, or Ascension) on the peak is evidence of a podium (possibly for a temple or shrine) of later construction. The summit commands splendid **views* over the whole of the island, which from here appears to be in the midst of a vast lake encircled by an almost continuous coast-line, formed by Attica, the Peloponnese and the islands of the northern Cyclades.

The asphalt road descends through Anitsaiou, to the seaside village of Portés, and turns north up the coast towards Aghia Marina. The pine trees on Aegina are generally very fine and full, but at Kilindras (2km north of Portés) they are at their best: their flowing volumes fill the valley.

The coast road south from Aegina runs past many beaches and improvised ports for small boats. At Prophitis Elias Bay, water coming down from Mount Oros has irrigated the whole valley, and the shore is backed with stands of eucalyptus and cane. On the low projecting spit of land at the southwest end of the island, the town of **Pérdika** has developed. There is a raised promenade of cafes and tavernas, where it is a pleasure to eat at sunset. From here it is possible in the summer months to take a boat across to the small **island of Moní**, which is less than 1km offshore to the west. The island has particularly clear waters in its bays, and the north side—where the caïques land—is well forested with pines. There are a number of protected species of animal on the island.

ANGISTRI

Angistri makes a delightful excursion from Aegina, although it can also be reached directly from Piraeus. The
island is a hilly protrusion on the Aegina shelf, separated
from the main island by subsidence. The shallow waters
and sandy sea-bed between Angistri and its own off-
shore islets of Metope (to the north) and Dorousa (to the
south), mean that the sea is of a limpid, tourquoise colour. The island's mantle of pines has survived well, and its
beaches are attractive.

   In the waters, 5km to its west, lies the uninhabited
island of *Kekryphaleia*, where according to Thucydides
(I, 105), the Athenians prevailed over a Peloponnesian
fleet in a sea battle in the early 450s BC. Pliny (Nat. Hist.,
IV 12.57) gives Angistri the name *Pityonesos* ('island of
pines'). The current name, *Ἀγκίστρι*, means a 'fish-hook'.
Throughout its history, which has closely followed the
vicissitudes of Aegina on which it has always depended,
Angistri has been alternately inhabited and deserted in
different periods. The ancestors of the present inhabitants are mostly Albanian Christian settlers from Northern Greece. In the late Middle Ages they fled Serbian in-
cursions to settle in the Peloponnese. They subsequently

came from there to the islands in the Saronic Gulf seeking refuge from Turkish dominion in the Morea.

Arriving boats stop mostly at the harbour of **Skala** at the northeast corner of the island. To the south, the road leads to the steeper and more dramatic east coast of the island—the bays of Sklíri (0.5km), with several hotels, and the more untouched **Chalikiáda** (1km), backed by pine-fringed cliffs. To the west, the road leads in 2km to the principal settlement of **Megalochóri**, also called 'Mylos'. On the hillside to the south of the road to Megalochori, is the island's oldest and most appealing settlement, **Metóchi**, embedded in the pine-woods that cover and scent the higher slopes. Terracing and walling in the valley below dates from the 18th and 19th centuries, and the centre of the village still preserves many stone houses from the same period. The other village originally settled on the island was **Limenária**, 5km to the south of Megalochori across the forested and panoramic ridge of the island, passing above the bay of Drangonéra. This southern half of the island has no hotels, and remains very tranquil. Limenaria, attractively sited on a plateau above the cove of Mariza, has the appearance of a Peloponnesian village, with many older stone houses. The wider landscape of the southwest corner of the island at **Apónisos** (1.5km west of Limenaria), with its small seasonal lake, reedbeds, and the off-shore island of Dorousa, is a good place for seeing a variety of migrating birds in early spring and autumn. For somewhere so close to the capital, the area feels remarkably remote.

PRACTICAL INFORMATION

180 10 **Aégina** or **Aígina**: area 77 sq.km; perimeter 56km; resident population 12,716; max. altitude 531m. **Port Authority**: T. 22970 22328. **Travel and information**: Karagiannis Travel, T. 22970 25664, www.aegina-travel.com

180 10 **Angístri**: area 11sq. km; perimeter 17km; resident population 886; max. altitude 275m. **Port Authority**: T. 22970 91541. **Information**: www.angistrigreece.com

ACCESS

By boat: Access to Aegina is by ferry or hydrofoil from Piraeus (Port Authority, T. 210 459 3123). By hydrofoil (*Hellenic Seaways*, T. 210 419 9000), the journey takes 35 minutes, with between 6 and 10 departures per day from Piraeus. Several shipping companies ply the short journey (1.5hrs) with car ferries to Aegina, in total providing departures every one to two hours throughout the day. There are also once daily services (more frequent in summer) from Piraeus to Aghia Marina in the east of the island. Most services leave from Akti Miaoulis in Piraeus, opposite the Electric Train terminus.

Hellenic Seaways operates a daily ferry from Piraeus (Gate 8) to Angistri, with frequency increasing to twice daily in high season. The caïque, *Angistri Express*, departs four times daily from Aegina for Angistri (journey time, 15 mins), with reduced frequency at weekends.

LODGING

Aegina: The **Aiginitiko Archontiko** is a small hotel (12 rooms) with great charm, in a neoclassical house opposite the mediaeval Markelon tower in the centre of Aegina town, on Thomaïdou Street. Its reception rooms are of historic interest. The personnel is helpful, and the atmosphere welcoming: open all year round. (*T. 22970 24968, fax.* *26716, www.aeginitikoarchontiko.gr*). More modern, with more space and easy parking, and not without charm, is the **Hotel Danaï**, just north of the archaeological site of Kolona in Aegina. (*T. 22970 22424*).

Angistri: One simple and comfortable solution for lodging is, **Rosy's Little Village** (*T. 22970 91610, info@rosyslittlevillage.com*) on the hillside at Skliri Bay. More institutional, but with more facilities, is the **Hotel Andreas** (*T. 22970 91346, fax 91231*) above the harbour of Skala.

EATING

Aegina: For the freshest fish and wine, in a simple setting with much local atmosphere, the taverna **Agorá** is a pleasure at all times of year. It is situated under the makeshift awnings at the back of Aegina's fish market, one block inland from the waterfront after the Demarcheion. It generally has octopus and small shrimp that are as good as can be tasted anywhere in Greece. At Pérdika there are many tavernas along the raised promenade: one of them, simply called '**10**', has some of the freshest produce and best prepared dishes amongst them.

Angistri: The island has many good tavernas: for fresh, home-cooking and a good chance of local wines and cheeses from the Peloponnese, the **Parnassos** in Metochi, and **Tasos** in Limenaria, are much to be recommended. Both are traditional village tavernas.

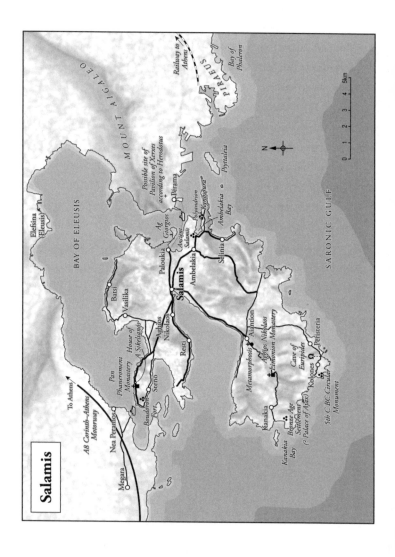

SALAMIS

The island's name is inseparable in the mind from the famous naval battle which took place in its waters in September of 480 BC, in which the fractious alliance of Greek city-states gained over the forces of Persia's King of Kings a victory, whose ultimate and far-reaching significance even they could not fully comprehend. To a people brought up generation after generation on the tales of the *Iliad*, the battle of Salamis, won against remarkable odds, was seen as the fulfillment of an almost heroic destiny and it gave the Greeks a confidence without which many of their greatest cultural achievements could not have been possible. The crossing alone to the island through the stretch of water where the battle was fought is a moving and thought-provoking experience, even though today it is a busy and densely inhabited artery of one of the largest ports in the Mediterranean, lined with ship-yards, warehouses and Greece's main naval headquarters. So close, in fact, is Salamis to the mainland and so integrated into the area's maritime industry that large areas of it are treated and inhabited as if it were a suburb of Athens, and its sprawling towns have much of the grating featurelessness which goes with that. The landscape is unmistakably

Attic, with wide treeless slopes, dusty earth and limestone outcrops over much of the island.

Fortunately Salamis is large and of unruly enough a shape to offer unexpected corners of tranquillity and relative beauty, especially along its south coast. Beyond the town of Aiantion—where there are a couple of interesting painted mediaeval churches—stretches a hilly promontory, forested with pines down to the shore at the attractive bay of Kanakia. In the last ten years, an important Mycenaean citadel has been uncovered on the hill overlooking the bay which with good reason can be believed to be the place where Ajax son of Telamon grew up, and from which he left for the siege of Troy, never to return. East of Kanakia along the south coast is the gloomy subterranean cave where Euripides is said to have retreated for peace and inspiration; and not far from it is a well-preserved circular building of the early 4th century BC which may possibly have been a mausoleum or *heroon*, impressively sited on a promontory commanding views over the Saronic Gulf. The island has attractive corners and plenty of interest, but because of its lack of hotels is probably best visited as a day excursion from Athens. This is easily accomplished since the island is so well connected by ferry at all hours.

HISTORY

In the 4th millennium BC when human habitation first began on Salamis at several identified sites, the island may have been a peninsula of the mainland, joined where there are now the shallow straits below Megara. With the development of seafaring and maritime trade in the Early Bronze Age (3rd millennium BC), settlement concentrated at a number of promontories on the island's south coast. At the beginning of the Mycenaean Age, one site emerged as the principal urban centre on the island: this was based around the citadel above the bay of Kanakia. It appears to have had wide-ranging commercial connections, which included Cyprus; it reached its zenith in the 13th century BC, but was destroyed and deserted by 1150 BC. It is probably the 'ancient city' referred to as the island's capital by Strabo (Geog. IX 1, 9). In the *Iliad*, Salamis contributed 12 ships to the Greek forces, led by Ajax, son of Telamon.

In historic times, the island first belonged to the city of Megara; but its control became the object of dispute between Megara and Athens in the time of Solon. It was annexed to Attica as a clerurchy by Peisistratos in the latter half of the 6th century BC, with the Athenians citing a forged line of Homer to support their claim. It was at this time that the capital was moved from the southwest to the east coast of the island—today's bay of Ambelakia. In the late summer of 480 BC, the Athenians evacuated their city in the face of Xerxes's push south after Thermopylae and made Salamis their base, trusting to the 'wooden walls' of their ships as the Delphic Oracle had advised them to. The battle fought in the straits between the east coast of the island and the Attic mainland was the most significant naval victory of early Greek history, and one of the most decisive for the course of Western history. The island later became a battleground twice during the course of the Peloponnesian War in 429 and 405 BC, but remained in Athenian hands through the 4th century BC, until it surrendered to the Macedonian commander, Cassander, in 318 BC. The island was restored to Athens again by Aratus in c. 230 BC. The Aianteia, a cult festival in honour of Ajax, continued to be celebrated on the island into the Roman period. Byzantine churches and spolia from the 12th to 15th centuries on Salamis suggest an intermittent continuity of habitation, but there is a lack of written notices of the island in this and subsequent periods.

PALOUKIA, SALAMIS AND THE EAST OF THE ISLAND

The short journey from Pérama in mainland Attica to Salamis passes to the south of the islet of Aghios Giorgios in the middle of the straits. The brief crossing cuts right across the heart of where the Battle of Salamis took place and gives a vivid sense of the cramped space in which the fateful encounter occurred: that confinement of space was something which was an important objective of Themistocles's strategy and which worked amply to the advantage of the much smaller forces of the Greeks. The **islet of Aghios Giorgios** would at that time have been almost attached to the main island of Salamis, separated by a shallow channel which was possibly even fordable. Today, its houses have been abandoned since the islet became part of the naval military zone which spreads along the shore to its north.

The ferry-landing is in the harbour of **Paloúkia** on the east side of Salamis, where a fleet of as many as twenty of the ferries that ply the crossing can be lined up along the quay at any time. The road north from Paloúkia leads into the Greek Naval Headquarters and is off-limits to visitors. This prevents access to what was probably the site of the temple of Athena Skiras, which is known from written sources: the terrace of the sanctuary constructed in polygonal masonry and some scattered architectural remains are on the south slope of the northernmost rocky escarpment which lies within the compound. Paloukia itself blends seamlessly across a shallow saddle with the town of **Salamis** (formerly called 'Koulouri') which spreads around the head of the bay of Koulouri. Its long waterfront on the north side of the bay in turn blends into the coastal settlement of **Aghios Nikólaos**. These are not ancient settlements, but suburban developments built hastily in concrete over the last seventy years. The centre of morning activity is the vibrant **fish-market** which takes place in a custom-built market-house on the north promenade: Salamis has one of the largest fishing-fleets of any island. About 800m further west along the waterfront is the large church of Aghios Nikolaos: directly to its west is the old **Archaeological Museum** in a small, one-room, concrete shelter, whose display cases exhibit Mycenaean artefacts found on the island, Classical and Hellenistic pottery from Ambelakia, and several carved grave stelai. (*At the time of writing the museum is in the process of relocating to three rooms in the former First Capodistrian Public School of Salamis. For up to date information telephone, T. 210 465.3572*) Many of the most important finds from Salamis, however, are displayed in the Archaeological Museum in Piraeus.

The **ancient city of *Salamis*** lay 1km to the south of Paloukia, beneath the modern settlement of Ambelákia, reached by taking the coastal road south from the point of disembarkation. The city overlooked a deep bay formed by the pensinsula of Pounta to the north and the long, straight projection of land called the Kynósoura ('dog tail') to the south. In the northwest corner of the bay can be seen the partially submerged moles of the **ancient harbour**. On the southern slope of Pounta (to the north of the bay) a section of the **ancient fortification wall**, made in mud-brick on stone, can be seen underneath a protective roof. The city has not been fully explored; but an *agora* framed by porticos, an altar to the Twelve Gods, a temple of Artemis, a theatre, and a Sanctuary of Ajax, are all referred to by Pausanias or in other written sources and inscriptions. Though vestiges of the town's Hippodamian plan have been revealed by scattered excavations, most of it still remains to be uncovered.

The main road which descends from the central square of **Ambelákia** towards the southeast passes (left) the attractive 15th century chapel of **Aghios Ioannis Pródromos**, which possesses a **painted iconostasis in masonry** and remains of late mediaeval murals in the apse. The tiny, rectangular interior is surmounted by a transverse barrel-vault. On the south side of the bay, as the road climbs over a low ridge, a left turn leads down the long **Kynósoura** peninsula, stretching over 2km out into the strait towards the Attic coast. On its north side, 1km along the headland beside the entrance to a large ship-yard, is the ancient *polyandrion*, or communal grave, of the Greeks who fell in the Battle of Salamis. The mound is clearly visible, overlooking the straits where the bat-tle took place and directly opposite the south slope of Mount Aigaleo on the mainland, where Xerxes reput-edly sat watching the rout of his fleet. Though marked today with a recent monument (2006), little remains of any comprehensible ancient structure, although in antiq-uity a trophy had been set up nearby, connected to a cult of Zeus. Below the circumference of the mound graves have been found of the late 5th century BC. Plutarch says that another trophy was set up on the **islet of Psyttaleia** which lies just off the tip of Kynósoura to the east, half way between Salamis and Piraeus. The islet played an important role in the Battle of Salamis: a Persian force of infantry, evidently comprising many aristocrats, was stationed there by Xerxes, which late on in the battle was annihilated to a man by Athenians under the command of Aristeides. Ancient writers refer to the islet as a place of worship of Pan; but today, its entire surface has been artificially levelled so as to accommodate the largest sewage processing plant in Europe. The identification of the reef as the Psyttaleia mentioned in ancient sources has been disputed in the past. The islet's modern name is Lipsokoutali, meaning something akin to a 'broken spoon': this is probably a corruption of a Venetian version of the name as '[L]i Psoutali'.

The ridge of Kynosoura is a good point from which to view the area where the Battle of Salamis took place.

THE BATTLE OF SALAMIS

The naval battle was fought in late September 480 BC between the forces of the Persian King, Xerxes I, and an alliance of mostly western Greek city-states led by Sparta and Athens. Xerxes hoped to subject and punish the Greeks, especially the Athenians, for their part in the Ionian revolts of the previous decades, and to avenge his father's defeat at the Battle of Marathon in 490 BC. Our primary sources for the battle are two: Herodotus in Book VIII of *The Histories*, and *The Persians* of Aeschylus. Herodotus's account is vivid and anecdotal, but short on exact detail of the battle: most later accounts, including Plutarch's in his *Life of*

Themistocles, closely follow his account. Aeschylus's dramatic version was first performed in 472 BC. Since he and most of his audience were present at the battle, we must assume his information to be the most correct and accurate.

The Persian strategy: Xerxes's faith throughout this whole, carefully-planned campaign was in victory through his overwhelming numerical superiority. That superiority in land forces remained intact, but his naval advantage had been considerably eroded by the severe losses inflicted at the Battle of Cape Artemision (Euboea) in August, where Greek ships had cleverly prevented him seeking safe-haven in a storm and turned the weather to their advantage. He had lost a large contingent of his navy; but it still numbered about 600 ships—twice the 310 which the Greeks could muster. His greatest disadvantage, however, was that time was against him: the campaign had taken longer than expected, and the Greeks had once again deliberately delayed him, at great cost to themselves, at Thermopylae. He had probably lost ten days there alone, and the summer was turning to autumn by the time he reached Athens in the second week of September. He needed to get the bulk of his forces and ships back to the Hellespont before the contrary winds of the new season set in. He could not delay for long, and the Greeks knew that. He had achieved his principal goal, which was to raze Athens; but that was a hollow victory, because he had been able to take no Athenians. They had evacuated the city in haste after Thermopylae: the women and children were mostly staying as refugees at Troezen on the east coast of the Peloponnese; the men and their ships had withdrawn to Salamis. He had scotched the snake, not killed it; and it was essential to his plan that he should eliminate the Greek military capability before he turned back to Asia. It would also have been risky for him to head for the Peloponnese, leaving the Greek navy intact, at his rear. He was under pressure therefore to face them and eliminate them, as soon as possible, before the weather deteriorated.

The Greek strategy: Themistocles, the chief strategist of Athens, knew that a confrontation of land forces would be doomed because of the numerical inferiority of the Greeks: at sea the situation was slightly better, since the loss of some of Xerxes's ships at Artemision. He knew that the Persians still had a navy twice as big as the Greeks, so it was essential that any confrontation happened in a confined space and not in the open sea, so as to minimise the Persian advantage of numbers. The straits of Salamis were ideal for this strategy. But two problems remained: how to draw Xerxes into the narrows in the first place against his better judgement; and how to keep the fractious alliance of Greeks together, without the Peloponnesian contingent sailing for home to protect their territory at the more easily defendable isthmus of Corinth. The solution was the same for both: to precipitate action as soon as possible. Themistocles knew that Xerxes must have been aware of the dissent in the Greek camp. According to Herodotus, he played on this and sent a secret message with his most trusted servant to Xerxes saying that the Greeks were preparing to flee, and that if he attacked them before they left the closed area of the Salamis waters, Themistocles would now come to his assistance. It was not the first time that a Greek 'bearing gifts' had been believed, not feared. In response, Xerxes first planned to build a pontoon of boats across the straits, but the attempt was foiled by Cretan archers. He then prepared for naval action, sealed both ends of the Salamis channel, and proceeded into a carefully constructed trap which was to lead to his defeat.

The battle: The Greek ships were beached along the east coast of Salamis from Ambelakia bay, north past the island of Aghios Giorgios and beyond. They numbered around 310 according to Aeschylus, more than half of which were Athenian. The Persian ships, numbering probably c. 600, were to leave their station in Phaleron Bay and to form at the south and east of the entrance to the straits around the island of Psyttaleia, with the prize Phoenician contingent at the fore and the less reliable Ionian Greek fleet at the rear. A squadron of Egyptian ships was dispatched to circle the island and seal the western end of the straits. Under cover of darkness, crack Persian infantry troops were landed on the islet of Psyttaleia. Xerxes, according to Herodotus, then took up a position on a throne to watch the action from the lower slopes of Mount Aigaleo (modern Pérama). On the morning of (?) 22 September, the Persians hoped to

surprise the Greeks at dawn; but Aristeides who had
arrived during the night at the last moment from Aegina brought news of the manoeuvres, and his account was confirmed by a ship from Tenos which de-
fected from the Persian side. The Greeks took to the
water at first light, singing their hymn, or paean, to
Apollo. Their right wing advanced first (Aeschylus),
probably so as to put themselves in a preparatory position to ram the Persian vanguard from both front
and side. Meanwhile the Corinthian ships which
were behind made a feint to the north (Herodotus)
as if they were fleeing, apparently confirming to
Xerxes what Themistocles had leaked to him about
the dissent in the Greek camp. This drew the Persian ships deeper into the channel. As they entered,
the fifty ships of Aegina and Megara, hidden to the
side of the channel in the bay of Ambelakia, attacked
them in the flank and rear. The narrow and confined
area of water meant that the Persians had great difficulty in responding and manoeuvring, especially as
the pressure of reinforcements, entering the straits
from behind, further clogged the area. As Themistocles had wished, a large part of the fleet of Xerxes was

rendered irrelevant, because it was unable to reach the theatre of action.

The battle lasted the whole day. In the late morning a wind blowing from the north down the channel favoured the Greeks and increased the disarray of the crammed Persian forces as they were pushed back on themselves, inflicting almost as much damage to their own vessels by retreating as the enemy did by advancing on them. The wind and rougher water upset the aim of the Persian archers, and favoured the armed hoplites of the Greeks who boarded and fought at close quarters. Xerxes could possibly have sustained the loss of so many ships, were it not that, late in the day, a force under Aristeides landed on Psyttaleia and decimated the Persian troops stationed there by Xerxes. Aeschylus describes the attack, and as an infantryman himself, he may have wanted to emphasise the particular contribution of his class of soldier; but if, as he says, these were Persian aristocrats—called 'The Immortals'—who were killed, this may have been the element which, combined with the rout at sea, decided Xerxes to return to Asia within days of his defeat.

The consequences: The Greeks, even before the time of Herodotus, had tended to define themselves in contradistinction to the Persians. They learned many things from the far older civilisation of the Persians; but much of their early history is shaped by their struggles against it—both in the Persian Wars of the early 5th century BC, and the later campaigns of Alexander the Great in the 4th century BC. By the time the two sides met in the waters of Salamis, Greece and the Greek identity had already emerged as something sophisticated, independent and highly individual, containing the germs of what was to become a distinctive, Western civilisation. Its survival depended on its freedom and independence; and in 480 BC that was threatened with subjection and possible extinction under Persian rule. The victory at Salamis, which ensured its survival, is seen with some justification by historians as a significant turning point in the history of the ancient world. It certainly gave the Greeks the kind of confidence on which great achievements are founded.

South of Kynosoura is the bay of **Selínia**, where a grid of streets inland from the beach accommodates a number of attractive **neoclassical villas** dating from the first decades of the last century. The resort looks across the water to Piraeus with Mount Hymettus behind.

THE NORTH OF THE ISLAND

Both **Batsí**, to the north, and Aghios Nikolaos and Stenó to the west of Salamis town are quiet coastal settlements of suburban homes with gardens, occasionally offering beaches for bathing in the protected waters—in particular along the north coast at Psili Ammos and Vasilika. The main monument of the area is the **monastery of the Panaghia Phaneroméni** (the Apparition of the Virgin), towards the western extremity of the north coast, 6.5km from Salamis—an interesting architectural ensemble dating from 1661, when the current building was founded by Hosios Lavrentios (the Venerable Laurentius of Megara), replacing a much earlier church on the site dedicated to the Metamorphosis.

The church clearly has a long history: the **carved *anthemion***
of a *stele* in the courtyard to the south of the church may
indicate an ancient structure on this site, while a number of
Early Christian spolia (such as the two column-stumps supporting the machicolation above the main entrance to the
monastery compound) point to it subsequently having been
occupied by an Early Christian building. The later, mediaeval **carved plaques of marble**, which were closure panels
from a *templon* screen, immured in the west façade of the
catholicon along with several fragmentary ceramic bowls in
the pediment, suggest that a new church was then built over
its foundations in the 14th century. The final rebuilding of
the monastery in its present form after 1661 follows western,
rather than Byzantine, canons of architecture: the high interior dominated by the long axis of the nave and the articulated and pedimented **façade** would not be out of place in
Italy. The **interior decoration** is pure Byzantine, however—a
(now very darkened) masterpiece of late Byzantine painting
in which the scenes and figures are perfectly disposed across
the architecture according to the canonical iconographic
plan. This is the work of the painter, **Markos of Argos** and
was completed in 1735, after the founder's death in 1707. The
chapel of Aghios Nikolaos immediately to the south (curi-
ously separated from the main *catholicon* by a steep staircase
which ascends to the belfry between the two buildings) con-

tains the tomb of Hosios Lavrentios. Its sober façade in white marble, with a wide *mezza-luna* above the door, framed by a simple cornice and the row of carved rosettes above, also show a strong Italian Renaissance influence. The monastery buildings became a refuge for women and children during the 1821 revolution and functioned as a hospital for the injured soldiers of the Greek army. Though founded as a male monastery, it became a convent for nuns in 1944.

Before leaving, it is worth noting the **main doors** to the monastery, constructed with wooden beams and revetted in bronze on the exterior. The original, swinging and sliding cross-beam for barring the gate is still in function. The exterior is dressed with a wide frame in Pentelic marble.

At the shore below the monastery, a small memorial bust commemorates the life of the poet **Angelos Sikelianós** (1884–1951); the solitary house on the water's edge to the east, recently restored, was his last home. Sikelianos was an exceptional lyric poet, whose poems can have an often oracular intensity and beauty to them. He was also a playwright, and friend of Nikos Kazantzakis. He revived the 'Delphic Festival' at Delphi in 1927, in a conscious attempt to reunite modern Greek culture with its ancient roots, and was a nominee for the Nobel Prize for literature. He is one of the most distinctive voices of 20th cen-

tury Greek poetry and deserves to be better known than
he is.

A kilometre and a half west of the Phaneromeni Monastery is the landing stage of the ferry-crossing to Nea
Péramos (for Megara and Corinth) on the Attic coast opposite. On the hill directly to its south, an ancient enclosure wall has been identified as belonging to the **fort of
Boudoron,** built by the Athenians during the Peloponnesian War as a defensive position to keep a watch on Megara, and mentioned more than once by Thucydides. There
are also the vestiges of two other ancient watchtowers in
the area overlooking the straits.

THE SOUTH OF THE ISLAND

AIANTION AND KANAKIA

From the junction beside the modern town hall of Salamis,
a road leads along the south shore of Salamis bay to **Aiántion** (5km). To the west of the centre of the village, which
is on the slope of the hill to the south, is the 15th century
church of the Koimisis tis Theotokou (Dormition of the
Virgin): 300m further west of this, partially built against

an outcrop of the natural rock below the pine woods at the upper extremity of the village, is the smaller *church **of the Metamorphosis**, which dates probably from the 13th century. It is a beautiful piece of architecture, unexpected in the context, and contains **wall-paintings** of several different periods. The steep cupola is supported on four monolithic columns with plain capitals in a cross-in-square plan. The *templon* screen is in masonry and painted with sacred images that have been damaged and partially retouched; there are also remains of wall-paintings of the 14th or 15th century in the apse, and of an almost life-size St George on the south wall. The paintings in the side chapel to the north are more complete, but darkened by candle-smoke and soot. Some of the windows of the church—one of which has a *bifora* design with central mullion—are still glazed with alabaster.

From the church of the Metamorphosis a scenic route climbs up through extensive pine forests with good views over the island and the Attic mainland beyond; once over the watershed, the monastery of **Aghios Nikolaos 'Limonion'** (9km) comes into view, hidden in a wooded fold of the valley below the road. (*Open daily from sunrise to sunset, except 1–4.*) The core of the original out-buildings of the 17th century is partly ruined, and a new extension has been built to the south by the nuns who now inhabit the monastery. In the centre of the compact courtyard is the *catholicon* whose dark interior has icons and an iconostasis of interest. The entrance-door in the north wall is flanked by two finely carved, marble *templon*-panels immured to either side of the entrance; these must have been saved from the previous, 12th century church on the same site. Above the door a masonry niche, with an inset Rhodian-ware dish, is decorated with a clumsy image of St Nicholas; above it, a curious **fragment from a 4th century BC funerary *stele*** with a banquet scene and a sacrifice at an altar, has been immured with the date 1740 scratched on its surface—the date presumably when the restoration of the monastery was completed. A short distance to the southeast of the monastery on the hillside opposite is the isolated church of **Aghios Ioannis Kalyvitis** dating from the 15th century. The interior is plain apart from vestiges of 17th century painting in the apse, but the well-proportioned exterior is attractive in its solitary setting. The stonework is interleaved with brick tile. The overall design of the building plays interestingly on contrasts between exterior and interior forms: the cupola-drum, which is cylindrical on the inside, is of square form with chamfered corners on the exterior; the three hemi-cylindrical lobes of the floor plan, are straight-edged on the exterior.

From the Monastery of Aghios Nikolaos, the road continues to descend through uninterrupted pine forest to the southwest shore of the island at **Kanákia bay** (13.5km)—a sandy cove with a small settlement and an offshore island in the bay. One of the most important, recent finds in Mycenaean archaeology has been made in this tranquil location. Archaeologists have good reason to believe that what they are unearthing may be the **city and palace of the Aiacid dynasty**, to which Ajax, son of Telamon, one of the most important of the Greek warriors mentioned in the *Iliad*, belonged.

The main area of excavation is along the ridge of the slope that rises to the south of the flat alluvial valley behind the shore. (*On arrival at the waterfront, turn left and continue south along the shore; then turn left again into the pine trees before reaching the small harbour. The site is on the summit to your left as you walk inland to meet the path leading up.*) The citadel and settlement, which grew into the island's principal urban centre, was continuously inhabited through the Middle and Late Bronze Age, but was then abandoned in the first half of the 12th century BC around the date that is generally ascribed to the siege of Troy. Looking across into the Peloponnese, with a protected harbour and a small fertile valley below, the city was well placed to play a leading role in the commerce of the Saronic Gulf. Finds made at the site bear witness to commercial links and contacts with other Aegean centres, Cyprus and even Egypt. The settlement conspicuously lacks the massive fortifications we find at Tyrins or Mycenae, but the buildings and the urban plan are created with a notably fortified aspect nonetheless—densely built and with substantial wall-foundations, and the bases of complex gates and towers. If this citadel was the home of Ajax, it is likely that he was the last king to live here: he never returned to it after leaving for Troy where, according to Sophocles, he died from his own hand. The city was abandoned shortly after. A cult to Ajax in historic times is attested on Salamis.

FROM AIANTION TO PERISTERIA

From the centre of Aiantion a road crosses the island to the attractive beaches and inlets of the island's south coast. At the southern extremity of the island is the bay of **Peristéria** (10km), fronted by two small off-shore islets. From a point shortly before the western end of the bay, a track leads inland, up between houses to the 'Cave of Cychreus', now generally referred to as the '**Cave of Euripides**'. (*The track soon becomes a steep path through pines and thorn bushes: the climb takes 20 minutes from the shore. A torch is essential for exploring the cave; and* *some head protection is advisable.*) Before reaching the cave the path passes the foundations of the walls of **two small shrines** which may have been related to the cult of Euripides and of Dionysos in later Hellenistic times; the threshold block and the plan of the eastern shrine can be clearly seen. The **cave** is a short distance above, entered by a long (c. 70m), low, serpentine passageway which is cramped and airless and not for the faint-hearted. It opens eventually into a broad, low-roofed chamber, forested with thick stalagmites and stalactites. The Roman author Aulus Gellius accurately described the interior as a '*spelunca taetra et horrida*'.

The cave has been investigated archaeologically (Prof. Yannos Lolos), and has yielded evidence of Neolithic use in the late 5th to early 4th millennium BC. One of its deepest recesses later functioned as a burial place in Mycenaean times. It acquired its name as the 'Cave of Euripides' thanks to a consistent tradition that the tragedian, who may have been a native of Salamis, used the cave for a period as a place of retreat. The finding of a fragment of a glazed cup dedicated with the name '*ΕΥΡΙΠΠ* [*-ΙΔΗΣ*]' (sic) suggests that the tradition has a long history: the inscription of the name dates probably from the 2nd century AD, and should be seen in the context of a later cult of the poet at the site.

At the western end of the bay of Peristéria, the road climbs
up over a hill and drops down into the village of **Kolónes**;
visible, in silhouette against the western horizon, on the
summit of the next promontory projecting into the sea
is the doorway and lintel of a curious structure dating
from the late Classical period. The building, constructed of large quadrilateral blocks of limestone, is circular
(about 8m in diameter) with an entrance and monolithic
lintel on the north side: in the interior are three neatly cut
and finished sarcophagi sunk into the ground, still *in situ*.
Both the width of the diameter, and the lack of sufficient
fallen masonry, suggest that the building was not intended to be a tower, or to stand more than about six courses
of masonry high at the most. Its purpose may have been
more akin to the so-called 'Tomb of Cleoboulos' near
Lindos on Rhodes to which it bears many resemblances.

PRACTICAL INFORMATION

189 00 **Salamis** or (more commonly) **Salamína**: area 91sq.km; perimeter 108km; resident population 34,975; max. altitude 365m. **Port Authority**: 210 467 7277. **Information**: www.salamina.gr

ACCESS

By boat: Car and passenger ferries make the 15-minute crossing between Paloúkia on Salamis and the port of Pérama (1), 8km to the northeast of Piraeus throughout the day and night: every 15 minutes from 5 am to midnight, and every hour thereafter. There are also ferries every 30 minutes to and from Paloúkia and the main port of Piraeus (2), between 6 am and 5 pm: on Saturday and Sunday afternoons the frequency drops to an hourly service. There is a car-ferry connection from the western end of the island which crosses every 30 minutes, between Stenó Phaneroménis (3) and the harbour for Megara, also confusingly called Nea Péramos: this then connects easily with the main Athens to Corinth highway. If you require your own car on Salamis, which is necessary for exploring the island properly, it is advisable to rent from Athens, since there is no obvious rental facility on Salamis.

LODGING

Salamis has only three, strictly utilitarian hotels. The nicest is the **Hotel Votsalakia** (*T. 210 467 1344, fax 210 467 1432*) on the waterfront at Selínia: it is welcoming and has its own good, restaurant/taverna. Of the other two, both in Aiántion—the **Hotel Gavrïel** (*T. 210 466 5748*) and the **Melina Resort Hotel** (*T. 210 464.0562*)—neither is recommendable except in an emergency.

EATING

A wide variety of dishes is offered by **To Pirophani** on the promenade road from Salamis towards Aghios Nikólaos. Further east, in Aghios Nikolaos itself, is the **Chris-tos** taverna for good fresh fish. The taverna of the hotel Votsalakia in Selinia is also to be recommended; and, on the waterfront below the 'Cave of Euripides' at Peristeria, is a small and anonymous fish taverna with a friendly host and freshly prepared, simple dishes.

FURTHER READING

The essential sources for the Battle of Salamis are: Aeschylus, *The Persians*; Herodotus, *Histories* VIII, 40 & ff; Plutarch, *Life of Themistocles*, 9 & ff. The selected poems of Angelos Sikelianos, finely translated by Edmund Keeley and Philip Sherard are published by Denise Harvey (Publisher), 34005 Limni, Evia, www. deniseharveypublisher.gr

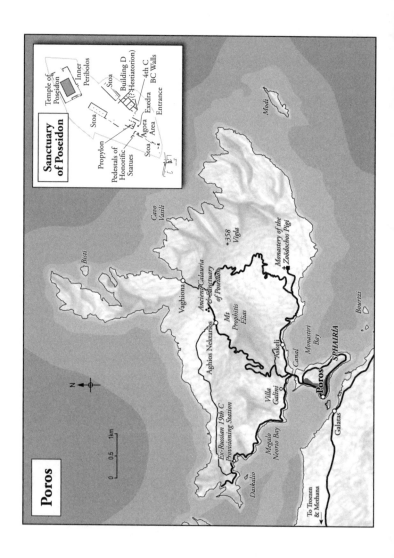

POROS

From across the narrow channel that separates the island from the Peloponnese, Poros still has the appearance, in the early morning light, of a watercolour scene by a 19th century traveller such as Edward Lear. The timeless charm of the island has been well conserved, with its picturesque architectural uniformity, the simple harmonious forms against the back-drop of pine-clad mountains—white and red against green—and the constant, unobtrusive activity of boats and caïques in its placid waters. The landscape is typically Peloponnesian, just as that of Salamis is typically Attic. Though small, the island has always had a certain strategic importance. In early antiquity the sanctuary of Poseidon on the island's central mountain was the focus of the Calaurian League, a confederation of important cities which included Athens and Aegina amongst others, all of whom were bound by a common need to pay due respect to the god of the waters on whom their life depended. The archaeologically explored area of *Calauria* and its sanctuary is still limited, but its panoramic setting is beautiful. Two and a half thousand years later, Poros was again a maritime centre and home to the first naval headquarters of independent Greece. The wealth that maritime trade has brought to the island is reflected in its dignified architecture.

The island is small and little built-up, making it easy to explore on foot or by bicycle; its waters are clean and its shaded coves a pleasure to bathe in. The town is compact and busy and, because of the ease of access from Piraeus, can occasionally flood with visitors during the day. But the mainland opposite, with its contrasting vastness, lies only 250m away and offers much of interest, both in history (Ancient *Troezen*) and in landscape (the monumental citrus groves of Galatas, and the dramatic Methana peninsula).

HISTORY & LEGEND

A large Early Helladic II settlement on the northeast coast shows that the island (or peninsula, as it then was) played an important role in the Saronic area as early as the mid-3rd millennium BC. Late Mycenaean settlement is also evident both on the islet of Modi to the east of Poros, and at the site now occupied by the sanctuary of Poseidon on the central heights of the island. According to Pausanias (*Descrip.* II 33, 2), *Calauria* (the ancient city of the island) was originally sacred to Apollo at the time when Delphi was sacred to Poseidon; the gods then agreed to exchange possession of the two places. Both Delphi and Calauria went on subsequently to become important centres of '*amphyctionies*' or sacred confederations. On Poros the cult of Poseidon was of primary importance and the island became the focus of the Calaurian League—an association of important cities which included Athens, Aegina, Epidauros, Hermione, Nauplia, Orchomenos in Boeotia, Prasai in Attica, and the nearby city of Troezen to whose territory the island belonged. The sanctuary of Poseidon at Calauria offered asylum; Demosthenes when pursued by Macedonian agents of Antipater, sought refuge here in 322 BC before committing suicide. In Late Antiquity an earthquake caused subsidence of the land, and the sea channel between the Peloponnesian coast and Poros was formed.

The island knew a period of growing prosperity after it was settled by Orthodox Albanians in the 17th century. In 1828, plenipotentiaries from France, Russia and Britain met on Poros to settle the terms and basis of the new kingdom of Greece in the so-called 'Protocol of Poros'. Three years later, the independent islanders, under the leadership of Hydra, took up an attitude of open hostility to the government of Capodistrias and established a 'Constitutional Committee'. The national fleet of Greece, including the frigate *Hellas*, its flagship, and the steamship *Karteria*, lay in Poros harbour. Capodistrias gave orders for them to be made ready to blockade Hydra; but Admiral Miaoulis, acting under the orders of the Hydriot government, preempted the move by seizing the fleet and the arsenal. On 1 August 1831, however, Miaoulis was overpowered by combined Russian and Greek forces. In the skirmish, he blew up the flagship *Hellas*, and the corvette, *Hydra*, rather than hand over the fleet to Russian Admiral, Pyotr Ivanovich Richord, as had been demanded.

Changes in the levels of water and land in what is a seismically very active area (witness the volcanic cone of Méthana visible to the northwest) have altered the geographical configuration of Poros. Today the island consists of two parts: the small, volcanic island of **Sphairía** (named after Sphaeros, the charioteer of Pelops) occupied by the town of Poros; and the main, mountainous body of the island, called *Calauria* in Antiquity, to its north. These are joined by a swampy isthmus today, but were separated by water in ancient times. The name 'Poros' means 'crossing' or 'ford'. Sphairia, on the other hand, was originally joined to the Peloponnesian mainland until seismic subsidence in Late Antiquity sundered it and created the shallow channel (only 250–300m wide) between Galatás and Poros. The islet of Sphairia in effect 'changed sides'. All this activity has resulted in a landscape of particular beauty, embellished by the simple, dignified architecture of 19th and early 20th centuries, set amidst pine-clad slopes and stretches of open water.

POROS TOWN

The elegant town of **Poros** is an architectural unity of prevailingly neoclassical style: the buildings cascade attractively down a steep hillside overlooking the channel, punctuated at the summit in the centre by the **clock-tower** of 1927. The buildings are cut and terraced into the native, trachitic rock—a stone of volcanic origin, whose colour varies from grey, to a deep maroon with something of the appearance of porphyry. The older houses are built in un-plastered stone, with a severe simplicity similar to the mansions of Hydra: the early 19th century **Deimezis mansion** set on a castellated parapet overlooking the waterfront from on top of a scarp of rock is a good example. With the accession of King Otto in 1832, a more explicitly classicising style became popular, and it is from the second half of the 19th century that the **Syngrou school-building** (opposite the Galatás ferry quay)—thought to be based on a design by Ernst Ziller, a German architect

who worked extensively also in Athens and in Syros—
and many of the houses along the promenade, all date.
Though similar in concept to one another, these houses
vary considerably in their details—the often complex
wrought-iron balcony closures and the carved marble volutes supporting them, the variety of *acroteria* and decorated cornices, and the balustrades above the attic with
variously shaped and moulded terracotta supports.

The town was founded in the 17th century by Orthodox Albanian refugees, moving out from the Peloponnese.
The first area to be colonised was the plateau above and
behind the waterfront, from which it is reached by steep
flights of steps. Today it is an attractive network of narrow
streets dominated by the island's principal church of **Aghios Giorgios**. The church may well occupy the site of the
ancient temple of Athena *Apaturia*, whose cult here and at
Troezen on the mainland opposite was particularly associated with the enrolment of youths into *phratries* (quasi-
hereditary clans or fraternities). In the square behind the
church is the large communal **water-fountain and cistern**,
constructed in 1880 from local stone, furnished with marble spouts (now blocked). There are a number of interesting buildings in the area, most notably the custom-built
neoclassical shop on the south side of the square, which
is remarkably well-preserved both inside and out. The ma-

jority of the churches of Poros have been built in the last 200 years, and often fully decorated inside in the same period: one of the few that predates this period is the plain, 17th century chapel of Aghios Ioannis Pródromos at the summit of the town, 100m east of the clock tower.

The long, curving waterfront is punctuated with small squares: the **Town Hall Square** still preserves its marble water-fountain, whose design is inspired by the choregic monument of Lysicrates below the acropolis in Athens. To the east, also on the waterfront, is Korizis Square. Alexandros Korizis, born on Poros, was briefly prime minister of Greece through the difficult early months of 1941: when German forces finally invaded Greece in April 1941, the perceived failure led him to take his own life. On the west side of the square is the **Poros Archaeological Museum**—a small and interesting collection of material both from the island and from the wider area of Troezen and Methana. (*Open daily except Mon 8.30–3.*) Larger, stone items are exhibited in the ground-floor room; smaller items in the upper-floor room.

Ground floor: The collection of grave *stelai* of various periods is interspersed with a number of unusual items (*to left on entering*): a cast of the '**Stele of Troezen**'—the inscribed decree of Themistocles ordering the evacuation of Athens before the arrival of Xerxes in 480 BC: Troezen was the recipient of the majority of Athenian women and children. Beside it is a split limestone block with a fine Archaic, **relief of a hunting-dog**, depicted with almost oriental stylisation. The case against the right wall displays a collection of fragments of a *sima* and other architectural elements which still preserve their vivid ***painted decoration**. These come from the Archaic temples of Aphrodite *Akraia* at Troezen and of Poseidon at Calauria, and give a good sense of the arresting decorative colours and designs on ancient sacred buildings. The stone architectural elements exhibited at the end of the room also illustrate the subtler chromatic variety

of material which was used often in the same sanctuary or building: for example, the Doric capitals in both grey trachite, and in soft, beige poros stone, both from the sanctuary of Poseidon.

Upper Floor: The central case of **Mycenaean votive offerings** from Methana includes fine long-stem cups, figurines, terracotta oxen, riders on horses, and small models of thrones; many of these items were designed also to accompany the body of the deceased in the grave. A second case (*immediately right against the wall*) of **Mycenaean gold jewellery**, a bronze sword and arrow-heads, includes miniature **plaques of bone with incised designs** of considerable fineness. A separate case by the stairs displays an example of a 7th century silver coin, known as the **Hexagram** (six Byzantine grams in weight), found on the fortress-island of Bourtzi in the channel to the east of Poros. The coin bears the two portraits on its obverse of a magnificently bearded Constans II and his son Constantine IV. Hexagram coins, equivalent in value to half of a gold *solidus*, were first issued by Heraclius in the early 7th century as an attempt to tackle the inflationary economic problems of the Byzantine Empire and were used for paying mercenaries and overseas administrators. The finding of the coin on Bourtzi indicates that the ample harbours which Poros offered were probably garrisoned in Byzantine times.

Detour: From the waterfront, close to the museum, water-taxis ply constantly to and fro across the busy channel to Galatás. By crossing to the mainland, a visit to Ancient *Troezen* and the Sanctuary of Hippolytos can be easily made. Combined with the citrus groves of Galatás and the dramatic landscapes of the Methana peninsula, it constitutes an interesting excursion.

AROUND THE ISLAND

The main road north from the western end of the promenade leads past what was the first Naval Training School of the newly formed Greek State. Until the facilities were moved to Salamis between 1878 and 1881, Poros was Greece's Naval Headquarters. The *Progymnastirion*—the large neoclassical building between the road and the shore, originally designed as a summer residence for King Otto, is still used as a training centre for navy personnel. In the wide bay in front of the building, the Greek flagship, Hellas, was sunk by Andreas Miaoulis in August 1831.

THE BATTLE OF POROS, 1831

Links between Hydra and Poros were strong since both islands had grown prosperous on their merchant fleets, which had customarily gone about their business in virtual autonomy under Ottoman rule. Perhaps the strongest bond between the two islands was that (richer) Hydra used the sheltered port of Poros extensively for its fleet since its own habours were vulnerable to northerly and westerly winds.

In the aftermath of the battle of Navarino (October 1827), in which the Ottoman fleet had been defeated by the combined forces of the Russians, the French and the British, a split had occurred between those Greeks who saw greater freedom and safety in the protection of the British (Hydra and Poros), and the mostly mainland Greeks, under Capodistrias, who favoured Russian protection because of the historically close religious and cultural affinity with the country. In essence, wealthy Hydra and its ally Poros saw their historic independence under threat from the nascent Greek Government and the increasingly arbitrary rule of Capodistrias; while, on the other hand, Capodistrias, the Governor of Independent Greece, realised that Hydra had somehow to be neutralised and its open hostility defused.

In the summer of 1831 the small and heterogeneous navy of the Greek State—less than a dozen large vessels—was in the port of Poros under the command of Constantine Kanaris. Capodistrias had given orders for him to use the fleet to blockade Hydra and restore control of the waters. Hydra learned of this and dispatched the veteran Admiral, Andreas

Miaoulis—by now a national hero—to counter-attack and take control of the navy. On 14 July 1831, his Hydriot forces together with sympathisers on Poros, took the fleet and captured the strategic islet of Bourtzi. The allies that Capodistrias could most rely on where the Russians, part of whose navy was still in the Aegean and constituted a force that it was difficult for Miaoulis and his supporters to resist. Open hostilities broke out in the last week of July, with the Russian Admiral, Richord, and a detachment of Greek army regulars under Colonel Kallergis taking Poros, recapturing the Bourtzi and sinking one of the vessels in the hands of the rebels—the corvette, *Isle of Spetses*, which formerly had been Laskarina Bouboulina's celebrated flagship, *Agamemnon* (see below p. 163). On 1 August, Miaoulis, rather than be forced to hand the ships over to the Russian command, detonated and sank both the corvette '*Hydra*' and the flag-ship of the fleet, '*Hellas*', subsequently slipping through the Russian lines unnoticed and returning to Hydra. In the mayhem that ensued Poros was looted and plundered by Kallergis's men.

The responsibility of Miaoulis's actions takes some

justifying. The Greek navy—of which Miaoulis himself had been such an important element—was small and in its infancy: his actions left it toothless and dependent once again on its powerful allies. Such a situation, which in his view might lead in the long run to a fairer and more stable solution for Greece, and particularly for Hydra, could well have been his strategic objective. He was 63 years old at the time and an almost unassailable national hero on the basis of his previous actions in the struggle against the Ottoman fleet. He survived to be made a rear-admiral of the navy once again in the new kingdom of Greece before his death only four years later.

After crossing the bridge over the artificial canal which separates Sphairia and Calauria, the road branches (1km). *The left branch* leads to Megálo Neório, passing below the russet-red **Villa Galini**, a fine example of a neoclassical rural mansion on the hill above, and then by the *Poros Image Hotel*, constructed in 1967 as part of the *Xenia* group, by one of Greece's best-known architects of the post-war period, Aris Konstantinidis. The road subsequently follows a succession of sandy coves, fringed with pines, the most intimate of which bears the name 'Limáni Agápis' or 'harbour of love'. The next bay west (3km) contains the unexpected ruins of a once grand piece of industrial architecture. The bay was used as a **provisioning station for the Russian Navy**; the two blocks—offices and quarters (near the shore) and store-houses and barracks (behind)—were built in 1834 by prisoners taken at the Battle of Poros. The Russian Navy maintained a presence in the area for almost a century—from the 1820s until 1917, when the station was abandoned and destroyed by the departing crews who returned home in loyalty to the Bolshevik cause.

Off-shore can be seen the islet of Daskalio—its pine-trees and the church of the Panaghia occupying nearly all of its surface: it is a popular place for weddings. Beyond, the pine woods of the south coast give way to a rockier landscape covered in low scrub and maquis. The road first heads north, and then climbs east: at 10km, it rejoins the main asphalt road, below the Sanctuary of Poseidon (*see below*).

The right branch by the canal follows the south coast, east through the pleasant resort of Askeli, to the 18th century **monastery of the Zoodochos Pigi** (5.5km), whose buildings are set a little way in from the shore, on a hillside above a densely treed valley with a running stream—the 'Life-giving Fount' of the dedication. (*Open daily 7–*

sunset, closed 1.30–4.30.) In front of the west door of the *catholicon* are several conspicuous gravestones to members of the Hydriot naval families of Miaoulis and Tombazis; beside them is the grave of Brudnell James Bruce, grandson of the 9th Earl of Kincardine. He died on Poros of a fever while accompanying the historic mission to Greece in 1828 in which Russian, French and British diplomats met on the island to consider the formation of an independent Greek kingdom. Another gravestone with an elaborately designed, classicising entablature is laid in the floor of the portico of the church. The *catholicon* itself is simple and undecorated, but is dominated by the magnificent ***wooden iconostasis**—a fine and well-preserved work of the 17th century, which predates the building in which it stands. Above the architrave are two levels of attic: *Scenes from the Life of Christ* below with a variety of figurative designs, reflected and balanced by an upper level with *Saints* disposed in pairs. The iconostasis was brought from Asia Minor, and may well be of Constantinopolitan workmanship.

THE SANCTUARY OF POSEIDON
'KALAUREATAS'

From the junction 1km west of the monastery the road into the interior of the island climbs through pine forests and crosses the central ridge of the island (10km), at which point the north coast and the long peninsula of Cape Achérado are visible below, with the island of Aegina clear on the horizon ahead to the north. At the coast below is the attractive inlet of **Vaghioná**, which can be reached by an un-surfaced road: visible under the water of the bay, when calm, are the outlines of buildings of a now submerged settlement. Due east, at the coast, is **Cavo Vasíli** where a substantial Early Helladic settlement of the mid 3rd millennium BC with the well-preserved bases of houses has been brought to light. It is the largest prehistoric site on the island to have been explored so far. On the islet of Modi, off the island's east coast, a Late Mycenaean settlement has also been identified.

At 12.5km, on a saddle between two hills, with ample **views** north across the gulf towards Attica, is the **Sanctuary of Poseidon** (*always open, though enclosed*). The site is tranquil and beautiful, but the paucity of remains do not do justice to the importance which the sanctuary had through much of Antiquity. Ongoing excavations by the Swedish Institute are uncovering significant new elements of the site however.

Layout of the site. As you stand at the entrance gate, with the sea ahead to the north, the area of the **sanctuary** extends to your right, with the site of the temple of Poseidon itself marked by a stand of pines in the top, right-hand corner of the area. Behind where you are standing and up the slope of the hill to your left was the Ancient **city of *Calauria*.** A **spring** (now dry) which may have fed the town and sanctuary can be made out low down on the slope of the hill just above the modern road to the left. The city has not been archaeologically explored; the only part of it which has been partially excavated is ahead and to the left within the enclosure, where the remains of an important public building have been identified. The most recent excavations are under the metal roofing, immediately in front of you and to the right.

History. The earliest excavations carried out by Swedish archaeologists in 1894 showed that the precinct was built on the site of a sanctuary that dates back to Late Mycenaean times (11th century BC). There was continuity of cult again from the 8th century BC; by the 7th century the sanctuary became the centre of the 'Calaurian League' whose mem-

bers included the powerful cities of Aegina and Athens. The
league is better termed an *amphictyony* since its bonds were
primarily cultic, and only secondarily military or commercial. The Temple of Poseidon and the precinct walls were
built at the end of the 6th century BC; the area was enlarged
again to the extent that the visitor sees today in the late 4th
and 3rd centuries BC. The sanctuary provided asylum: it
functioned as a place of inviolable refuge for suppliants, the
most famous of which was the orator Demosthenes (*see below*), who sought sanctuary here from Macedonian pursuit
in 322 BC. His tomb was honoured by the Calaurians.

The remains are not easy to read.

- Ahead and to the left is the area believed to correspond
  to the agorá of the city of Calauria; it is bounded (back
  left, beyond the olive trees) by a long **stoa with slightly
  protruding wings** at either end, dating from the 4th
  century BC. Near to its right-hand end are many pedes-
  tals for honorific statues of benefactors.

- Ahead and to the right is the sanctuary itself, which was
  defined to south by a precinct wall or *peribolos* laid in
  the 6th century BC. This is obscured by the large additions which were made in the 4th century BC, when a
  building of triangular plan was added to its south: a
  magnificent stretch of its wall is visible right in front

of you, constructed in parallel rows of 'ballooned' lime-stone blocks, drafted at the edges. This structure (Building 'D') is divided into rooms and may have functioned as a ritual dining area or *hestiatorion*.

- The precinct proper was entered from a point 30m ahead of the entrance, where the rectangular base of a (4th century BC) ***propylon*** can be seen, preceded by a small, circular stone structure with what looks like a stone bench against its interior wall: this was in fact an ***exedra*** (probably for statues) of slightly more than semicircular form. East of the propylon, a large esplanade of trapezoidal form opened out, bounded to left and right by long ***stoas***—two contiguous stoas to each side—whose bases are visible. These were covered porticos with Doric columns. From inside this area the triangular building 'D' can be seen more clearly.

- At the northern end of the area stood the Temple of Poseidon, built around 520–510 BC—a Doric, peripteral structure in limestone with 6 x 12 columns. Nothing of it or of its altar remains because the stones were carried off and used as building material on other islands in the early 19th century; but its plan can be read from the foundation works in the ground. The surrounding **inner *peribolos*** in rough stone, with two entrances, one to the east and one to the south, can be seen clearly. The temple would have been visible from far out to sea. Its position commands the waters to the north, as if looking from a crow's nest with the promontory below extending like the long bow of a ship.

DEMOSTHENES'S LAST DAYS

Demosthenes was one of the greatest intellectual figures of 4th century Athens—a statesman of almost obsessive energy, with a passionate devotion to the cause of liberty and to his city. His orations are justly considered works of art and monuments to the cause of freedom. He was neither the first nor the last great Greek to run foul of the tragic inability of his fellow Greeks to unite properly in the face of perceived danger from outside. His implacable hostility to the threat of Macedonian nationalism and the expansionist ambitions of its king, Philip II, has seemed to some a heroic idealism and to others a dangerous allergy to pragmatism. After Philip's death in 336 BC, Demosthenes played an important role in his city's uprising against Alexander the Great. His efforts were doomed, and the victory of Alexander's viceroy, Antipater, at Crannon in 322 BC led to the imposition of a Macedonian garrison on Athens. Demosthenes was condemned to death by a decree of Demades, and fled to Calauria to avail himself of the asylum offered by the Sanctuary of Poseidon. He committed suicide there by taking poison in the autumn of 322 BC. The Calaurians honoured his memory with a tomb which was seen by Pausanias (*Descrip*. II 33, 3) within the precinct.

From the village of Aghios Nektarios, 1km below the archaeological area of Calauria, the road crosses the shoulder of Mount Prophitis Elias, and returns to the canal and to Poros after 6.5km.

PRACTICAL INFORMATION

180 20 **Póros** (ancient name, Calauria or Kalaureia): area 22sq. km; perimeter 42km; resident population 4,182; max. altitude 358 m. **Port Authority**: 22980 22274. **Travel information**: Saronic Gulf Travel, T. 22980 24800, fax 24802, www.saronicgulftravel.gr

ACCESS

By boat: Poros is well connected by fast services in the summer, with typically 3 connections a day by Hydrofoil, three by fast Catamaran, and two by larger ferry, most of which ply the whole route from Piraeus to Poros, and on to Hydra, Ermioni, Spetses and Porto Heli. Between mid-October and Easter the service reduces significantly, with the regular ferry providing the main communications. These services are all run by one company: *Hellenic Seaways* (www.hellenicseaways.gr). The car and passenger ferry from Galatas on the mainland opposite makes the five-minute crossing every 30 mins.

LODGING

The **Hotel Dionysos** (*T. 22980 23511*), on the waterfront opposite the Galatas ferry landing-stage, is a simple dignified traditional guest-house in a mansion of 1826, with inexpensive rates. The *Hotel

Roloi (*T. 22980 25808, www. storoloi-poros.gr*) offers beautifully appointed apartments for longer stays and is situated in the oldest part of the town above the harbour front. For luxury accommodation, open year-round, the ***Poros Image Hotel**, in a 1960s building designed by Aris Konstantinidis, provides every comfort and service, as well as superb views (*T. 22980 22216–8, fax 25725, www.porosimage.gr*): it is 2km outside the main town at Neorion.

EATING

In the upper town, the taverna **Platanos**, near church of Aghios Giorgios, set back under a pergola beside the 19th century water-cistern, combines a peaceful setting with good, traditional Greek food.

FURTHER READING

For the Battle of Poros, a fundamental source is George Finlay's *History of the Greek Revolution*, first published in 1861, now reprinted in two paperback volumes, published by Elibron Classics (2005).

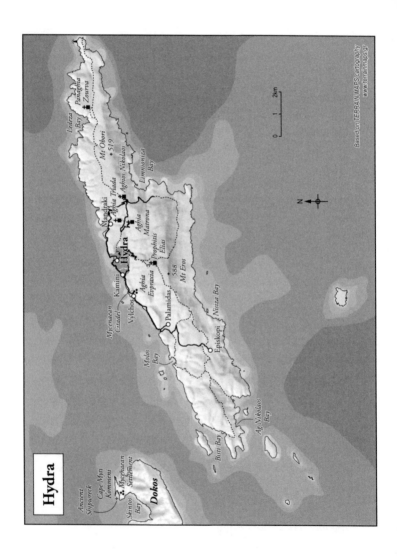

HYDRA

At the turn of the 19th century, when Athens was home to about 6,500 inhabitants, the population of Hydra may have exceeded 30,000—nearly five times its size. Today its residents number less than 3,000, while in Athens they now exceed five million. The demographics are important for understanding Hydra and its history and architecture. Maritime Greece, with its fragmented geography of islands in the sea, has always been an interconnected network of moderately small comparable entities. Hydra was for a while an important player in this constantly changing map of evolving and declining centres. The island (like Chios before it and Syros and Symi after it) came into a period of remarkable prosperity at the end of the 18th and the beginning of the 19th century, when it was a magnet for commercial shipping interests in the Aegean area. The parallel is perhaps closest with Symi, which like Hydra was a mountainous rock in the sea with no extensively cultivable terrain: both islands were thrown back onto shipping and commerce in order to survive. The sudden growth of wealth has produced in both islands a narrow period of extraordinary architectural flowering, endowing them both with ports that are among the most strikingly beautiful in the Aegean.

Hydra is the only island in the Aegean in which the municipal authorities have had the tenacity to maintain a total ban on motorised traffic. It is one of a very few places in Europe where this is the case, and it has transformed the quality of life on the island. As a consequence, Hydra is a dense urban tissue but with none of the negatives which that normally implies. The interior of the island is also only accessible on foot, and in recent years a growing monastic community has returned to Hydra to take advantage of the peacefulness which that has brought.

Proximity and fast communications to Athens mean that visitors often come to Hydra merely for a day's excursion. But—not least because it has a number of very beautiful hotels and guest-houses—it is an island that should be visited for several days so as to savour both its extraordinary tranquillity and to explore its uncompromised wealth of architecture. Hydra has few 'great buildings' as such, but it is one of the best preserved and least modified architectural and urban 'wholes' in Greece and should feature in any serious traveller's first acquaintance with the varied beauty of the Greek Islands.

HISTORY

Archaeologists have located as many as a dozen sites dating from the Early Helladic II period (2800 to 2300 BC) mostly on headlands and promontories around the coast of the island, showing that Hydra was substantially settled in prehistory. The main, proto-urban centre in this period was on the plateau of Episkopi. In Late Mycenaean times the island was an outpost protecting and supplying the maritime trade-routes to the centres of the Gulf of Argos, with a fortified citadel above Vlychos and a supply station near Cape Bisti. There are few references to Hydra in early historic times, apart from a mention in Herodotus (III, 58.) which states that the island was purchased in around 526 BC from the people of the mainland city of *Hermione* by a detachment of exiled Samians, opposed to the rule of Polycrates. Insufficient water may have been the reason for the island's lack of settlement in later antiquity. In view of this it is curious that the names '*Hydra*' and '*Hydrea*' in Antiquity, clearly cognate with the ancient Greek word for water, '*ὕδωρ*', should have been given to an island with exceptionally little water. Evidence of prehistoric works to store and manage water at a site near Cape Bisti (*see below*) suggest that water was probably once more abundant than now. But even the presence of minimal fresh water on the island may have had a greater significance than usual on Hydra in antiquity, because the island served as a point of replenishment for boats on the sea routes in this area. This may be how it earned the name it now possesses.

During the 16th and 17th centuries refugees from Turkish rule in mainland Greece, of mainly Christian Albanian descent, settled on the island. On Hydra, they became practically self-governing, paying no taxes but supplying sailors to the Turkish fleet. In the late 18th century their merchant fleet grew rapidly and prospered on the trade of corn from the Black Sea, which Hydriot ships supplied to French markets by skillfully breaking the British blockade imposed during the Napoleonic Wars. By the time of the outbreak of the Greek War of Independence in 1821, Hydra had a population of over 30,000 people, and one of the largest merchant fleets in the Aegean. Just as in Chios, the council of elders that governed the affairs of the island at first vacillated at the outbreak of the revolutionary war, wary of imperilling their considerable prosperity and concessions from the Ottoman authorities in exchange for an uncertain future. But with the leadership of Lazaros Koundouriotis, however, who converted his fleet of trading vessels into men-of-war at his own expense, Hydra became the largest force in the Greek revolutionary navy and a fundamental contributor in the struggle for independence. Among the many Hydriot naval commanders of the war were Iakovos Tombazis, Anastasios Tsamados, Dimitrios Voulgaris and Andreas Miaoulis, the commander-in-chief. The war resulted in independence for Greece; but it caused the depletion of Hydra's wealth, resources and manpower. A further economic blow came with the arrival of steamship transport which rendered obsolete what remained of the Hydriot sailing fleet. The commercial activity of the Aegean moved to other islands, Syros and Andros, and Hydra never recovered, suffering an unrelenting emigration of its population through the late 19th and early 20th centuries. The fine urban, architectural heritage of the years of prosperity was little by little abandoned. Only recently has tourism and new settlement, attracted by the island's tranquillity, begun to redress the balance, leading to the restoration of many of the buildings.

Architecture and history of the town

The *town and harbour of Hydra** only come into view
at the last moment, hidden in a deep breach in the wall
of limestone slopes which constitute the north coast of
the island. The harbour is a tight semicircle of deep water, able to accommodate boats of considerable draught:
protective spurs of rock rise steeply to both sides of its
entrance. The town is slotted into the small bowl behind
the harbour and up the lower slopes of the mountain
which rises steadily behind to its summit of 588m: it is
only saved from the summer heat, which this configuration would intensify, by its north-facing aspect.

Hydra is the most complete architectural unity in the
Aegean, comparable only with the port of Symi for ho-
mogeneity and dramatic setting. Almost the entire sweep
of the main town can be taken in from the point of disembarkation. Its unique and distinctive architecture is a
mixture of austerity and clean elegance. Façades are not
articulated, and are generally flat and rigorously symmetrical. Relieving arches are occasionally picked out over
windows but there is otherwise no decoration. Preference
is given to un-rendered walls of the local grey limestone.
The eaves are de-emphasised and scarcely project over the
façade: the pitch of the roof is consonantly low. The effect
of all this is quite distinctive: one of solidity, gravity and

seriousness, which the brilliant light of the Aegean alone succeeds in relieving. This is 'mountain-architecture' more than what we understand as 'island-architecture'. Its origins lie in the rugged mountains of northwestern Greece—the area from which a majority of the settlers on Hydra in the 18th century originated.

This beautiful and undisturbed ensemble of buildings, has been admirably conserved by the municipal authorities. The lack of traffic and its accompanying noise is a palpable release; but attention has also been paid to the elimination of visible concrete, of jarring signs, and of half-built structures which have tended to become the norm elsewhere. There are clean contrasts and a welcome clarity in what the eye beholds. A pleasant balance of vegetation and colour offsets the austere stone. The town and its setting are a humane space, a perfect solution to island living.

The development of the town of Hydra dates from the settlement of the narrow plateau, directly to the south of the port, which was referred to simply as *Kiafa*, or 'hill', in the language of the first Albanian stock-breeders and farmers who settled there in the late 17th century. As the economy increasingly came to depend on boats and trade over the next century, the building nucleus spread down the slopes towards the harbour and, with a rapidly increasing population, filled the area in between. An itinerary is proposed below which begins at the harbour, climbs up by the Koundouriotis House to the area of Kiafa, and returns by way of the wells at Kala Pigadia.

AROUND THE HARBOUR

At the northeast corner of the harbour are the fortified **batteries** of 1821, still furnished with some of their cannon. On the upper level is the bronze **statue** (1892) of **Andreas Miaoulis** by Konstantinos Kazakos; on the lower level, a bust Antonios Kriezis (1796–1865), a Hydriot naval commander who fought in the Greek War of Independence and was later Prime Minister of Greece, under King Otto, from 1849–54.

ANDREAS MIAOULIS, 1768–1835

Andreas Vokos Miaoulis, one of the most sympathetic and interesting figures of the Greek revolutionary war, was born on Euboea, but considered himself a citizen of Hydra where he settled and lived. He was a highly skilled mariner in the merchant navy and by the age of 17 had become captain of a commercial ship, acquiring considerable wealth in the corn trade through a series of courageous sea operations during the blockades and difficult conditions of the Napoleonic wars. In 1822 he was appointed Admiral of the heterogeneous Greek revolutionary fleet, which had been hastily improvised from converted merchant ships: over half the ships were from Hydra itself, and he would have been familiar with them at first hand. His first mission was the avenging of the Turkish Massacre of Chios in 1822. With far inferior resources at his disposal, he succeeded in harrying and impeding the movements of the Turkish and allied Egyptian navies. He played a crucial role in the relief of the first siege of Messolonghi in the winter of 1822/3. As the revolutionary war against the Ottoman Empire intensified, with the involvement of larger players—Britain, Russia and France—Miaoulis stepped back to allow one of the most successful and ingenious veterans of naval action of the time, Thomas Cochrane, Earl of Dundonald, to take command of the Greek navy. Dundonald was a colourful, talented, but controversial personality: he had been relieved, probably unjustly, from his command in the British Navy in disgrace, and had since acquired considerable experience serving with revolutionary fleets in Chile and Brazil. Perhaps there was something in the outspoken fearlessness and independence of thinking which the two men shared, that led Miaoulis to cede his control.

Miaoulis maintained an active role in Greek affairs after the War of Independence, and became involved in the open hostility of Hydra to the increasingly arbitrary power of the Russian-dominated faction of Ioannis Capodistrias, which threatened Hydra's prominent position in Greek maritime affairs. At the instigation of the Hydriot council, in a daring act of what was in effect sanctioned terrorism, Miaoulis forcibly took control of the Greek Fleet in the harbour of Poros in July of 1831, and in August destroyed two of its ships, including the flagship *Hellas*, rather than hand it over to the Russian command as Capodistrias had requested (see *Battle of Poros*, pp. 108–111). Shortly before his death, he was once again appointed Vice-Admiral of the Greek Navy. His heart is preserved in a small shrine in the Museum of Hydra.

The large building overlooking the harbour, just south of the battery, houses the **Museum of Hydra**, a full and well-displayed collection of memorabilia of Hydra's maritime glory. (*Open daily 9–3.*). The prevailing spirit of nostalgia, and the flamboyance of the naval personalities and events which the museum commemorates, are an illuminating contrast for the Anglo-Saxon visitor, accustomed to the different culture of imperturbability and 'stiff upper lip' in the northern European naval world.

Entrance foyer. Immediately left, by the entrance to the museum shop, is a display of **Mycenaean finds**, including the modelled head of a clay figurine of the 12th century BC from the Vlychos area. There are several **ancient amphorae** retrieved from the sea-bed around Hydra.

Upper floor: main gallery. The centre-piece of the room is the heart of Andreas Miaoulis conserved in a solid silver *lekythos*. Around the walls is a wide selection of portraits—many of the best painted by unknown artists—of Hydriot freedom-fighters and seamen; this complements the remarkable collection of earthenware plaques with portraits painted of the **'fire-brands' of Hydra**, which are assembled on the wall beside the staircase. 'Fire-brands' were the young men who hazarded their lives in the risky operation of attaching a fire-ship to an enemy naval vessel and detonating it, after making a rapid withdrawal to safety. This was the technique used by Constantine Kanaris to destroy the Turkish flag-ship at Chios: it became one of the Greek Navy's most powerful weapons. A large model of one such vessel—usually a converted type of a merchant brig—is displayed in the room adjacent to the main hall. The **ships' por-traits** around the walls have considerable variety—some documentary and detailed, others picturesque with often interesting light effects. Dominating the hall from the rear is an example of the inde-pendent **Hydriot Flag**—blue, with a white cross (faith and suffering), a snake (endur-ance) and an owl (wisdom).

The landing and back room exhibit a number of wooden **figureheads** and prow decora-tions. The cases display an im-portant **collection of swords and pistols**, and of ceremo-nial costumes, including an exquisite example of a *lady's embroidered over-gown, or cape, called a 'pirpirí'. At the top of the stairs are the origi-nal **18th century, wooden doors** and ceiling decorations from the Voulgaris Mansion.

From the promenade in front of the Museum several of the principal family mansions, or '*archontiká*', of Hydra can be seen. Immediately to the left, the next building along the harbour front, which now houses the Greek Merchant Naval Academy, is the Tsamados Mansion (c.

1790). This, and the **Tombazis Mansion**, directly across the harbour, are both tower-like constructions set within high enclosure-walls whose irregular contours, following the shape of the hill, contrast pleasingly with the severe rectilinearity of the buildings. The Tombazis *archontikón*, which is now home to a branch of the School of Fine Arts of Athens, has—as is often the case with Hydriot mansions built on the steeper slopes—several entrances on different levels: the principal one on the upper (fourth level) has a beautifully **carved marble surround**. Prominently visible to the right of the Tombazis mansion, dominating the hill which forms the western projection of the harbour area, is the classically pure, four-square **Voulgaris Mansion**, symmetrical and almost identical on every face: the only decorative relief is provided by the 'brows' above the windows. The mansion was built by Giorgios Voulgaris, Governor of Hydra between 1802 and 1812. Conspicuous by its distinctive yellow stucco and upper-floor loggia is the **Koundouriotis Mansion**, high up on the western hill to the southwest of the port: this, and the **Gouroyannis Mansion** (not visible from here: at the southeastern extremity of the town by the well-heads of Kala Pigadia), to which it bears many similarities, are probably the oldest of the *archontiká*, and date from the period 1780–90, when, with the increasing importance of the port and its ships to the economy of the island, the settlement began to fill the area below the plateau of Kiafa.

As you walk round the harbour-front, it is worth noticing the paving-stones of the **harbour esplanade**, which are in a particularly attractive local stone from the mainland opposite. It is a pale grey, brecciated, limestone, beautifully mottled with veins which vary from orange to russet-red. At the centre of the sweep is the clock-tower, behind which lies the island's **cathedral of the Dormition of the Virgin**. This was founded as an isolated monastery in 1643 by a nun from Kythnos, long before the town grew up around it. The present building dates from a renovation in 1776. A comment in the account written by Richard Chandler of the London *Dilettanti Society* of his journey to Greece in 1764–66, mentions his seeing stone and building material taken from the temple and sanctuary of Poseidon on Poros being shipped to Hydra for the building of monasteries on the island. Some may have been destined for this building. The monastery is entered through a vestibule leading into a light, airy, pillared courtyard on two levels. The portico of the church has finely carved (18th century) marble capitals: in front of it stand busts of Andreas Miaoulis and Lazaros Koundouriotis—the two most important figures from Hydra during the Greek War of Independence. These men and the council of notables who ran the affairs of the island met in the rooms of the monastery under the aegis of the church which played an important role in both the civil life of Hydra and in the revolutionary war. The interior of the catholicon is densely decorated, and is dominated by a complex and somewhat top-heavy iconostasis in marble. The monastery has a small **Ecclesiastical Museum** of liturgical items and icons of the 17th to 19th centuries. (*Open daily except Mon 10–5.*)

Of particular note are an 18th century icon of the **Virgin of the Roses** with contemporary, ornate frame, and a delicate 16th century image of Aghia Paraskevi, hidden in the farthest room of the collection. There are two good examples of 18th century **Ottoman firmans**, 'sealed' with the ornate, gilded monogram, or *tuğra*, of the Sultan. A curiosity of the collection is the strongly westernising image of the *Lamentation* (1770) on a rectangular panel of canvas, which functioned as an *epitaphios*—the banner carried in the Easter procession of Holy Saturday.

The offices of the Town Hall occupy a part of the Monastery buildings, including its principal reception hall which has a superbly **decorated ceiling**. It is possible to see this by asking at the Secretary's office on the first floor.

The streets that radiate inland from the esplanade all originated as torrent-beds for the drainage of water from the mountain, and still perform this function today when it rains. For this reason they are designed with elevated side-walks and deep kerbs. One of these, Votsis Street, passes to the west of the cathedral church, and opens out after 100m (heading away from the harbour) into **Votsis Square**, overlooked from the south by the dignified 19th century building of the *Hydroussa Hotel* (ex-*Xenia*) and from the west by the island's hospital. From the south side of the hospital, steps lead up steeply to the **Koundouriotis Mansion**, which is open to the public as a museum and historic residence. (*Open daily Apr–end Oct 9.30–3.30. Visits can be made at other times of year on request: T. 22980 52421, or 210 323 7617.*) The beauty of the house, which dates from c. 1780, lies mostly in the spacious proportions and elemental simplicity of its principal rooms and furniture—characteristics it shares with several of the houses of the founders of the early American Republic, whose tranquil atmosphere it recalls.

Lazaros Koundouriotis (1769–1852) was the leader and political representative of the principal families of Hydra in the period of the Greek War of Independence. He inherited a successful shipping and trading business from his father, and later committed a very large part of the wealth which it represented to the Greek revolutionary cause, its navy and its practical needs, from 1821 onwards. He furnished both ships and moral guidance to the independence movement. It is said that he only left the island of Hydra on one occasion. He had 14 children of whom eight survived to adulthood. Many of his descendants have been prominent in politics and in the Greek Navy.

The mansion: ground floor. The main entrance leads into a **courtyard** below the pillared loggia of the upper floor. It is often maintained that these early Hydriot buildings are built on designs by Genoese architects: the contrast here of the elegant loggia with the severe and undecorated exterior, is certainly northern Italian in inspiration. A number of Hellenistic and Roman **funerary** *stelai* and reliefs, probably found on the mainland opposite, are immured below the staircase to the right of the court. An airy yet stately *****vestibule** runs the width of the interior. Below its floor and that of the courtyard are large water-cisterns: the beautifully **carved octagonal drinking-fountain** above one of them stands to the right of the main door, supplying water directly to the area of the public rooms. This is a feature in common with many of the other larger mansions in the town. The main rooms leading off the vestibule are all characterised by high ceilings, fine proportions and a simplicity of furnishing in a mixture of Ottoman and Western style: the simple elegance of the **cypress-wood door-frames** and other fitments is notable. Placed above the east-facing door onto the verandah is the long panel of **family icons**. In the main hall is a full-length portrait of Lazaros Koundouriotis: the sash and cross have been added at a later date.

The upper floor rooms are grouped around a panoramic **loggia** of simple design, which commands views over the whole town and port: they contain a display of furniture and (mostly female) ceremonial **costumes* from different parts of Greece—elaborate and beautifully coloured skirts, and brocaded jackets. Those in the last room, representing the three 'naval islands'—Psará, Hydra and Spetses—are perhaps the most delicate of all. The bakery and cellars in the undercroft can also be visited, where a permanent exhibition of the works of the painters Constantinos and Perikles Byzantios (father and son) can be visited.

Directly above the Koundouriotis house is the church of the Ypapanti, or 'Purification of the Virgin'; by following the street as it climbs to the south amongst attractive houses, past the smaller churches of St Spyridon and then St. Tryphon, you come to a point where another street crosses at right angles. This is **Kriezis Street** which traverses the upper town from east to west, and leads down a shaded and broadening valley to the west, finishing at the shore once again at the fishing settlement of Kamini. Continuing straight on across Kriezis Street, you climb to the church of the **Tris Gerarches**, whose unappealing exterior is compensated for by an attractive 19th century painted iconostasis and marble floor-decorations in the interior. The area south of here is the heart of the original settlement of Hydra, called '**Kiafa**', which was first occupied in the early 17th century—if not before: it is grouped around what is probably the town's oldest church, **Aghios Ioannis Pródromos**. (*The church is c. 150m uphill to the southeast of the Tris Gerarches: the key is currently kept in the house immediately to the right of the western gate into the church's precinct.*) The original cross-with-dome design is from the 17th century, but the church was renovated in 1783. It is the only church on the island to have a complete cycle of **wall-paintings** in its interior: these date from the late 18th century as does the church's carved, wooden iconostasis.

By climbing a short distance beyond the church and then following the main path left, it is possible to descend from Kiafa to the east, towards **Kalá Pigádia**. As you descend the final stretch of stepped path, the large, yellow *archontikon* in the valley below, with a central loggia similar to that of the Koundouriotis house, is the **Gouroyannis Mansion**, whose construction also dates from c. 1780. The heterogeneity of its roofs and the irregular projection of the loggia give it considerable charm. The name 'Kala Pigadia' ('good wells') refers to the two ample **well-heads** around which the terraced square is constructed. These were dug under the governorship of Giorgios Voulgaris at the turn of the 19th century: together with the wells at Kamini, they were the principal source of water for the town of Hydra and supplemented the cisterns beneath every house which stored winter rain-water. Today fresh water is shipped daily to Hydra from the mainland.

From Kala Pigadia, the wide, stone-paved, **Miaoulis Street** leads downhill to the harbour again; its route is lined with substantial houses of the early 19th century, a couple of which are entered through colourful **neoclassical doorways**, added at a later date.

Alternatively, by circling the Gouroyannis Mansion and continuing to climb, you reach the monasteries above the town.

THE MONASTERIES OF PROPHITIS ELIAS AND AGHIA EVPRAXIA

(*Contrary to the indications given on most available maps and guides, this is not a '45 minute' walk, but an unrelenting, 75 minute climb.*)

Beyond Kala Pigadia, Miaoulis Street rises to the south; it becomes concrete, then gravel, then track, then path and finally steps, as it approaches the ***monastery of Prophítis Elías**. (*There are some signs; but, at any junction, always take the steeper uphill turning.*) Although a late construction (1815), the solitude of the site, the magnificent views and above all the serene simplicity and austerity of the architecture of the monastery amply repay the climb. The paved area enclosed by a low quadrangle of monastery buildings is silent and wide; at its centre, the *catholicon* sits isolated like a ship on a grey sea. Its outlines are clean, clear, austere—typically Hydriot. The pale stone-work, and the brilliant white pointing of the joints lends an icy detachment to the whole complex. The *catholicon* has pleasing proportions and compact volumes both inside and out. There is a wide range of 18th and 19th century icons in the interior, with one particularly powerful image of the Prophet himself in the south conch. On the

terrace outside the monastery, a chapel to the island's pa-
tron saint, St Constantine of Hydra, stands apart at a little
distance to the northeast. Not long after it was completed,
the monastery was used as a place of reclusion, and during the civil strife of the mid 1820s Theodore Kolokotronis was imprisoned here.

The *views are superb, encompassing the coasts of the
Peloponnese and Attica, and the islands of Aegina, Kea,
Kythnos, and (to the west) Dokos and Spetses. A short
distance below the monastery to the northwest, a stone
path leads down to the sister establishment of the **convent of Aghia Evpraxía**, which was built fifty years after
Prophitis Elias. Intimate, compact and burgeoning with
vegetation, the convent has a more feminine identity
which is a pleasing contrast to the austerity of Prophitis
Elias. Aghia Evpraxia, known as Saint Euphrasia in the
west, was a 4th century saint from a noble family related
to the Emperor Theodosius. She retired to the Egyptian
Desert with her mother and pursued a life of asceticism
and ministration to the needy. She died in 413 at the age
of 30: her feast is celebrated at the convent on 25 July.

The highest summit of the island, at Mount Eros,
588m, rises directly to the south, and can be reached by a
further 35 minutes' climb.

OTHER WALKS ON THE ISLAND

Hydra has no motorised vehicles, so exploration of its considerable length (20km from east to west) has to be undertaken on foot or by mule. The mountainous interior is grand and panoramic, but the walks are not bucolic: they are hard and mostly shadeless, especially in the east. There are no springs, so it is important to take drinking-water.

WEST: KAMINI, VLYCHOS AND EPISKOPI

(*Distances in time by foot from the main harbour*)

A stone-paved road leads from the port round the western battery to **Kamíni** (15 mins.), the attractive fishing harbour for Hydra. It is here, on Good Friday every year, that the *epitaphios* is borne in procession from the beach into the sea. The route continues for **Vlychós** (25 mins.), which sits at the mouth of a gorge, overlooked by rocky rises to east and west. The plateau of the eastern hill (101m) was occupied by an important **Late Mycenaean citadel** (13th–12th century BC), which overlooked the coast and the sea passage between Hydra and the mainland.

As you approach from the east, stretches of **fortification wall** in courses of rough masonry can be seen high up on the northeast face of the hill. The area at the summit shows evidence of settlement, with terraces below, and a gateway on the northwest side. Fragments of clay figurines (*see Hydra Museum above*) and lead-weights for fishing nets have been found on the site. Archaeological evidence shows a continuation of use on the site in historic times, which may corroborate an allusion made in Herodotus (*Hist.* III, 58–59), where he says that a detachment of Samians, having extorted a large sum of money from the people of Siphnos under threat, proceeded to buy the island of *Hydrea* from the city of Hermione. This hill-top was probably their garrison-post which would have been taken when, according to Herodotus, the Samians were trounced by the surprise attack of a force from the island of Aegina in c. 526 BC. Surface finds on the hill, of coins and arrow-heads, would appear to corroborate this.

At Vlychos the path crosses an attractive **arched bridge** built in dry stone according to the same design as the bridges in the mountains of Epirus which were built around the same time, at the end of the 18th century. At **Palamídas** (50 mins.) is a small boatyard which still functions today. Overlooking it from the east is the long

boat-house building in typical 19th century, Hydriot architecture, with arched boat-docks at ground level. The path—still a wide gravel road—rises into the interior from Palamidas, climbing through woods of Aleppo pine to a ridge with views down to the cove of Molos, and the former summer mansion of the Voulgaris family behind its shore. Shortly after the watershed, as the road descends to the south side of the island, you come to the half-inhabited, half-abandoned settlement of **Episkopí** (100 mins.). Surface finds in this area suggest that it was settled both in prehistoric times and later in the Roman and Early Christian period. The **church of the Koimisis tis Theotokou** has a forecourt with columns and spolia from an earlier Byzantine structure: the name 'Episkopí' could possibly be interpreted as suggesting an episcopal presence in Byzantine times. The village was favoured by Hydriots in the last two centuries as a retreat for its cooler climate in the summer and for hunting in the autumn. Today it is a settlement of scattered houses and chapels, olive groves and walled enclosures. A path continues for a further thirty minutes to the east of Episkopi descending to Nisiza Bay on the south coast.

Behind the Bay of Aghios Nikolaos near Bisti at the south-western extremity of the island (*reached by boat*), another interesting **Mycenaean installation** has been identified, dating from the 13th century BC. On the slope of the hill, at a point where springs must previously have existed, are the remains of terraces and walls of considerable height which appear to have been designed to store water, perhaps with the purpose of creating a supply station for the crews of passing ships, plying the trade-routes between the Argolid and the Islands.

EAST: MANDRAKI AND THE EASTERN MONASTERIES

A somewhat featureless, shoreline road from the east battery of the port leads in 20 minutes to the bay of **Mandráki**, which was the main harbour and ship-yard of the Hydriot fleet during the 19th century. The route passes the small church of the **Eisodia tis Theotokou**, or 'Presentation of the Virgin', above the shore, before the descent into the bay. In the hills above are three monasteries and nunneries—**Aghia Triada**, **Aghia Matrona**, and **Aghios Nikolaos**—which can be reached by following paths behind the bay, but which are more easily and pleasantly arrived at along the wide path which leaves the main town of Hydra from the cemetery in its southeastern corner (Aghios Nikolaos in 90 mins, the other two in well under one hour). From Aghios Nikolaos, a further two hours and fifteen minutes of rough track, round the north side of Mount Obori, brings you to the **monastery of the Nativity of the Virgin**, or the '**Panaghia of Zourva**'. (*In view of the difficulty of finding the outward route and the length of the walk, this monastery is best visited by taking a water-taxi from the port in Hydra to the Bay of Ledeza, where a path climbs up the cliff to the monastery in 40 mins: the return west across the island is more easily navigated.*) The isolated setting of the monastery is remote and panoramic. The walk to it, however, is shadeless, and a supply of drinking-water is essential: it takes just over 3 hours, one way. All of the above monasteries are 18th or 19th century foundations: Aghia Triada, 1704; Aghios Nikolaos, 1724; the Monastery of the Nativity, 1814; and Aghia Matrona, 1865. All have been meticulously renovated and re-inhabited in the last two decades after a period of abandonment. This flowering of monastic life on the island is due in large part to the absence of motorised vehicles on Hydra which favours monastic isolation and tranquillity.

The low, castellated **lighthouse of Cape Zourva**, at the eastern tip of the island was built in 1883. After its destruction during the Second World War, it was restored in its original form in 1949.

DOKOS

Four kilometres north of the western tip of Hydra is the uninhabited island of **Dokos**, Ancient *Aperopia*. (*Access only by private boat or water-taxi from Hydra.*) Lacking any satisfactorily sheltered port in its own coastline, Hydra used the protected bay of Skintos, which cuts deep into the north coast of Dokos, as its winter anchorage for the fleet. But the shelter of the bay has commended itself to mariners for several thousand years before. Evidence of this was the discovery in 1989 of the earliest **cargo ship-wreck** found so far in the Eastern Mediterranean area, in the waters just off the northeastern tip of the island near Cape Myti Kommeni. The ship, which foundered some time around 2200 BC, was carrying a cargo of vases, amphorae, and other terracotta items, such as braziers. Since then, excavations near to the cape, and at Lezeda on the north coast further to the west, have uncovered two important **settlements of the mid-3rd millennium** BC. Continuity was maintained into Mycenaean times: the extent of the remains of the two walled settlements which flourished in the 13th and 12th centuries BC, in tandem with the citadel above Vlychos on Hydra, shows that the waters of the Saronic Gulf have always had considerable importance, with key trade routes that go back to the 3rd millennium BC, and perhaps earlier.

PRACTICAL INFORMATION

180 40 **Ýdra** or **Hýdra**: area 49sq.km; perimeter 64km; resident population 2,629; max. altitude 588m. **Port Authority**: 22980 52279. **Travel and information**: Ydraïoníki Travel, T. 22980 54007, www. hydra.gr

ACCESS

Hydra has typically three connections a day by Hydrofoil and three by fast Catamaran, which ply the route from Piraeus to Hydra via Poros, and on to Ermioni, Spetses and Porto Heli: these are run by *Hellenic Seaways* (www. hellenicseaways.gr). For the reduced services between mid-October and Easter, which can sometimes be suspended in bad weather, it is best to visit the company's web-site. A fleet of water-taxis connect the port with outlying harbours and beaches around the island; and will also make the crossing to the mainland (Metochi, 20 mins) or to Spetses (45 mins) in most weather conditions. The price-list for these services is exhibited at the water-taxi station.

LODGING

Hydra does not have a large number of hotels, so it is a good idea to book ahead in high season, but they are of a notably higher standard and sense of style than elsewhere. At the top end of the scale, is the elegant *Bratsera Hotel, sensitively created and luxuriously appointed in a converted sponge factory (*closed only between mid-Jan–mid-February, T. 22980 53971, fax 53626 www.bratserahotel. com*); more traditional in style is the *Hotel Hydroussa (formerly Xenia) in the historic mansion on Votsi Square (*open Easter–Oct, T. 22980 53581–5, fax 52161, www. hydroussahotel.gr*). A middle-ranking hotel of great charm, in a converted private house, worthy of recommendation, is the long-standing * Hotel Miranda (*open March–Nov, T. 22980 52230, fax 53510, www. mirandahotel.gr*). At the less expensive end of the scale is

the **Piteoussa Guest House**— simple, yet with considerable old-world charm, and open all year (*T. 22980 52810, fax 53568, www.hydra.com.gr/ piteoussa*). All are in the lower part of the town, not far from the harbour: signs are very scarce on Hydra, and since you need to walk to the hotels with your luggage, these indications on how to find them may help to avoid unnecessary wandering. Bratsera and Piteoussa: take first turning in to left from southeast corner of harbour (Tombazis Street). After c. 100m the Bratsera is signed to your left. The **Piteoussa** is further on, on your left when you see pine-trees beside the street. **Hydroussa** and **Miranda**: follow harbour front round to right and take last turn in to left before clock tower. After '**To Steki**' taverna (100m), cross right into adjacent Votsi Square for **Hydroussa**, or continue 50m further to **Miranda**, on your right.

EATING

Eating can be surprisingly unimaginative on Hydra by comparison with the high quality of the island's hotels; there seems little ambition to do more than the regular fare. One of the nicest and most welcoming places, offering fresh and varying proposals in Greek cuisine every day, is **Kristina's** (properly '**Chrysina's**') '**Gitoniko**', in the alleyway close by, and to the right of, Stavros Douskos's long-standing and famous taverna, **Xeri Eliá**. The latter also has reliable food served on tables beneath the trees in the square; but it is a more commercial operation. **To Steki**, near Votsi Square, has straightforward fare, and an attractively 'un-reconstructed' interior with folk-murals of ships and boats on the walls. At Kamini (15 minutes' walk from the main harbour) **Kontylenia's** taverna, has pleasing views and some imaginative dishes.

SPETSES

As the first island in Greece to raise the flag of insurrection and to lead the others into the War of Independence which ultimately gained the country its freedom from Turkish dominion, Spetses holds a special place in the Greek imagination. The war in Greece was less than two weeks old when Spetses joined and its goals could not have been achieved without the vital contribution of the improvised navy which Spetses provided together with the islands of Hydra and Psará. A key figure in all this was Greece's national heroine, Laskarina Bouboulina, who from her base on the island made courageous inroads into the Ottoman hold on Greek territory. Her house is one of the monuments of Spetses. It and the many other large houses, nearly all dating from the 18th and early 19th centuries—including that of the family of Bouboulina's assassins—constitute the principal interest of the island and compose its urban landscape. It is a sober, classical architecture, similar to that on Hydra—only less concentrated and more scattered on Spetses. Cutting an unusual figure in the midst of this, are three conspicuous monuments of later date, built by the island's greatest benefactor, the tobacco magnate, Sotirios Anargyros, at the beginning of the last century—his neoclassical mansion, an élite school which bears his name, and a grand hotel which would not be at all out of place on the *Promenade des Anglais* in Nice. Anargyros was the first to see that, with the demise of its shipping fleet, the island's future lay in attracting a wealthy and cosmopolitan tourism.

Judging by the plutocratic estates along the island's eastern shore, and the yachts that arrive in its waters in the summer, Anargyros's wishes have been, in one sense, fulfilled. Spetses today is a place of contradictions, with widely diverging qualities of tourism and of architecture: the Anargyros buildings languish and decay while new, luxury housing flourishes; (non-resident) cars are banned, while fleets of motor-scooters create noise and disturbance in their place, sidelining the horses-and-traps which were so much a feature of the island's charm. Before the beginning of this century, the beauty of the island's crystalline waters and celebrated pine-forests could always be relied on: but devastating and repeated fires in the last fifteen years have left the tree-cover decimated. There is little now remaining still to be burnt, and it will need decades for the landscape to be restored to its former beauty, worthy of the island's ancient name, *Pityoussa*, meaning 'abundant in pines'.

HISTORY

The recorded history of the island is confined mostly to the last 300 years; though excavations by Dimitris Theocharis on the promontory of Aghia Marina have shown that there was a flourishing Early Helladic settlement on the island in the mid-3rd millennium BC, with some later occupation in Mycenaean times. In historic antiquity the island is mentioned by name as *Pityoussa*. The Italians gave it the name '*Spezia*' or '*Spezie*'—either in reference to the pungent pine- and herb-scented air ('spiced'), or to some perceived similarity with the verdant coast of La Spezia in Liguria. The island was settled during the 17th century by refugees from Turkish rule on the mainland. The abundance of wood both on the island and on the mainland favoured a flourishing industry of boat building. By the turn of the 19th century, the island's population was c. 18,000, and it possessed a large merchant fleet. The first open call in the Islands to revolutionary arms in the Greek War of Independence, was from Spetses on 3 April 1821. Spetses, together with Hydra and Psará—the three 'naval islands' as they are referred to—contributed the uprising's all-important navy. The island provided a number of prominent and successful naval commanders,

and the country's best-known heroine, Laskarina Bouboulina, who led her own ships in the siege of Nauplia in
1822. After the war, the arrival of steam-ships sidelined
Spetses and its fleet, and the island's economic situation
languished. At the beginning of the 20th century, a Spetsiot tobacco magnate, Sotirios Anargyros, returned to Spetses and put his wealth into projects for the island—roads,
aqueducts, an international hotel and an élite school—
laying thereby the foundations of a tourist industry which
sustains the island today. Devastating forest fires in the
1990s and in 2000 destroyed the greater part of the island's
celebrated pine woods.

The arrival at Spetses could not be more different from
Hydra. The island is low, green, and domesticated, with
a long straggling waterfront of miscellaneous buildings.
One looks in vain for a real 'centre' to the town because
Spetses has several centres. This is a function of its development over time. The built area spreads over the whole
of the northeast corner of the island. Before looking at
individual monuments, it is helpful first to understand
the overall development.

The historical development of the town and its architecture

Earliest settlement was at the far eastern extremity of the island where a creek cuts deep into the coast, with a protective headland to its east side. This is the **Old Harbour**, or Palaio Limani, where artefacts from the Roman, Early Christian and Byzantine periods, as well as Bronze Age remains nearby, show that it was used and inhabited up until the 8th or 9th century, when pirate raids led to its abandonment. It was not until 700 years later, in the late 15th century, that settlers from the Peloponnese returned to the island, building themselves a base at **Kastelli**—the rise which now forms the highest point of the town, directly south of the point of disembarkation. This was fortified with a wall in the late 17th century. As both security and prosperity grew with the establishment of the island's commercial fleet, the area of habitation rapidly expanded down the slopes towards the shore to the point now referred to as the '**Dapia**', where the ferries and hydrofoils arrive. The old harbour became an active boatyard once again, and the island's richer, merchant families built houses along the 1.5km of shore between the Dapia and the Old Harbour to its east, through the early decades of the 19th century. Later in the 19th century the stretch to the west of the Dapia was favoured and developed. Unlike Hydra there were no geographical confines to the space, and so the town extended freely in all directions. The early houses of the important families are built along Italianate lines, with loggias on their upper floors. The later *archontiká*, or mansions, were built to a more simple, symmetrical design, cubic in form with regularly spaced windows, as on Hydra. At first they had flat roofs, as elsewhere in the islands; but the influence of pitched and tiled roofs from the mainland of the Peloponnese soon prevailed. Greater colour and a whitewash to the walls is favoured on Spetses as opposed to the un-rendered stone which prevails on Hydra.

THE DAPIA AND THE HOUSE OF BOUBOULINA

All the boats dock close to the harbour of the '**Dapia**', which is about half-way along the three kilometres of waterfront. At the landward end of the harbour mole, the first building you encounter is the so-called '**Chancellery**'—a modest, symmetrical building in stone dating from the turn of the 19th century—whose name comes from the fact that it was the Town Hall and meeting-place of the island's elders at the time of the War of Independence. The harbour here is shallow and exposed, and the island's fleet principally used the Old Harbour; even so, the front at the Dapia is fortified, and some of its cannon emplacements remain. The name 'Dapia' comes from the Turkish word, '*tabya*', meaning a bastion or fort. Today it is a raised esplanade crowded with café tables and is the focus for the summer '*volta*'—the constitutional taken at sundown by Greeks in order to see and be seen. Overlooking the area is the statue of the island's heroine, Laskarina Bouboulina—portrayed in no mood for joking.

The **House of Bouboulina**, now a small, well-maintained museum, stands just across the street from the southwest corner of the Dapia. (*Open daily 25 March–31 Oct; visits are by guided-tours only, in either English or Greek, at times advertised at the entrance.*) The house, which dates from c. 1700, is still used by Bouboulina's descendants.

The building, enclosed in a walled-garden, must have stood on its own as a small rural estate in the early 18th century. It belonged to Bouboulina's second husband, Dimitrios Bouboulis. Its style is distantly Italianate, with the main reception rooms on the upper floor giving onto an **arcaded loggia**. The simplicity of the interior—as with the early mansions of Hydra—is again reminiscent of early American houses of the same epoch. The most ornate element is the magnificent *wooden ceiling in the main room, which is of Florentine workmanship, and Balkan-Ottoman design. Most of the furniture was of French or Italian origin—including an impregnable safe of remarkable ingenuity. In the upstairs rooms, which have been left as little changed as possible, are many of Bouboulina's memorabilia—her pistol, the Ottoman license for her ship, *Agamemnon*, bearing the imperial seal or *tuğra*, and a particularly beautiful head-scarf which she customarily wore. Only four rooms can be visited, but they give a clear sense of the tasteful and comfortable simplicity of well-to-do living in the Aegean in the early 19th century.

LASKARINA BOUBOULINA, 1771–1825

As the self-appointed commander of her own squadron of warships, an indomitable fighter, the only female member of the *Philiki Etaireia* (the secret society of Greeks living mostly overseas who were preparing Greece for its independence revolution), and the only Greek to be posthumously honoured with the rank of Admiral in the Russian Navy, Laskarina Bouboulina is one of the most remarkable figures of the Greek Independence struggle. She was

born of Hydriot parents in Constantinople during
the imprisonment of her father there by the Ottoman authorities for his part in the First Russo-Turk-
ish War. After his death she grew up with her mother
partly in Hydra, partly in Spetses. By the age of 40 she
had been married and widowed twice; she was left
with seven children, but possessed a considerable in-
heritance from her two husbands—which, although
threatened with confiscation on a political pretext
by the Turks, was eventually released after her deter-
mined appeals in person both to the Russian Ambas-
sador at the Ottoman Court, Count Stroganov, and
to the mother of Sultan Mahmud II. Whilst in the
capital she had cultivated her contacts with the *Philiki Etaireia* which encouraged her to continue her
preparations for the revolution. She purchased arms
and ammunition at her own expense and completed
the construction of her warship, the *Agamemnon*,
by bribing Turkish officials to ignore the fact that
it exceeded the dimensions permitted by Ottoman
law and flouted the restrictions on arming of craft.
She is said to have preceded the official declaration
of war by raising and saluting her own revolution-

ary flag as early as 13 March 1821. In action, she and the vessels under her command distinguished themselves against heavy odds at the blockades of Nauplia, Monemvasia and Pylos; she also participated together with her son at the siege of Tripoli in the Peloponnese, where—fulfilling a promise she evidently had made to the Sultan's mother—she succeeded in saving the women of the harem from the indiscriminate slaughter and reprisals following the fall of the city. Three years later, however, her opposition to the unwarranted imprisonment of Theodore Kolokotronis earned her the displeasure of the new Greek government, and she returned to Spetses rather than be arrested and imprisoned herself. She became embroiled in a feud after her son had eloped with the daughter of Christodoulos Koutsis, scion of another prominent naval family of Spetses, and was shot in May 1825, in a dramatic settling of domestic scores. Her flagship, *Agamemnon*, was donated by her descendants to the state and re-commissioned with the name, *Isle of Spetses*. It was destroyed and sunk by Andreas Miaoulis during civil strife in 1831 in the harbour of Poros (see '*Battle of Poros*', pp. 108–111).

THE BUILDINGS OF SOTIRIOS ANARGYROS

To the rear of the Dapia, a small attractively cobbled square opens behind, with the church of St Anthony on the right-hand side. At the far left corner is a bronze statue to one of the island's most important benefactors, **Sotirios Anargyros** (1849–1918), who returned to his native Spetses after accumulating a fortune in the United States from tobacco production. His signature-brand, *'Turkish Trophies'*, was bought by James Duke. The business, at the time of its sale in 1897, was worth the (then) immense sum of $650,000. (Ironically, the name 'Anargyros' means 'money-less'.) Before the outbreak of the First World War, Anargyros began a number of projects for the benefit of the island: he bought tracts of land in order to re-forest them with pines after decades of depletion from fires and timber collection for boat-building; he constructed the first fresh-water aqueduct, as well as the road which circles the island; and, with the building of the *Poseidonion Hotel*, he brought employment to the island and put Spetses firmly on the tourist map. His house, the ***Anargyros Mansion** directly across the street, is perhaps the island's most memorable building, completed in 1904 in high Neoclassical style, with 'Egyptian-ising' details such as sphinxes and palm trees. Beneath its elegant façade with fine classical door-frames, friezes and columns, its alternating pediments and segments over the windows, and its cadenced colour scheme, is a structure in concrete and iron—the first of its kind on an island whose tradition of building was with pure stone walls. The design is a curious hybrid: the central, cubic block of the house, typical of a neoclassical villa, is surrounded by a wide portico on all four sides at the lower level—an unusual feature that Anargyros had picked up from his visits to the 'ante-bellum' estates of the American South where his tobacco was grown. After Anargyros's death, the building served as a town hall, then as an interrogation centre during German occupation: today it moulders, awaiting a new project for its use.

The second of the great projects which Anargyros undertook was the **Poseidonion Hotel**, on the waterfront just to the northwest of the Dapia. The era when its faded elegance could still be enjoyed ended in 2003, when the hotel closed for lengthy renovation works. It was a curious idea—but once again of American inspiration—to build a luxury hotel of monumental proportions and of an alien kind of architecture, on a small island of the Saronic Gulf: but it enjoyed huge success and was patronised by

princes and potentates from all over Europe and by the
beau monde of Athens. In its heyday, after 1928 when the
British Fleet used Spetses as an anchorage and its clientele
was a mixture of Athenian society and British naval offic-
ers, it was the most important seasonal hotel in the Bal-
kans. Its architectural design, which is to be preserved in
the refurbishment, was modelled on the marine 'Hydros'
of northern Europe, in which wrought-iron balconies,
steep-pitched roofs, and pyramidal copper canopies to
the towers, brought a kind of Parisian metropolitan architecture to the sea-side. It was a piece of the water-front
of Le Touquet, in the Aegean. A date has not yet been set
for its reopening.

To the west of the Poseidonion is another large building of 1920, now converted into a luxury hotel ('*Nissia*')
out of what was originally the Daskalakis Textile Factory,
which operated for nearly 40 years until it closed in 1959.
The shore beyond it is fronted by simple dignified houses,
interspersed with archontiká: the building of the current
Demarcheion; the **Economou Mansion** (1851); and, in a
walled enclosure further to the west, the **Altamura Mansion**. At this point the area has ceased to be the munici-
pality of Spetses and has become **Kounoupítsa**. Behind
the high wall to the left of the road as it continues west
is the last of the great philanthropic projects of Sotirios

Anargyros—the ***Anargýreios and Koryialéneios School of Spetses***, which was completed in 1927 in a 'Rationalist' architectural style, typical of the epoch.

This was not intended as a school for Spetsiots, but for the wider Greek world. Its creation responded to a movement in the politics of the period, in which the '*Megali Idea*'—the 'great vision' of a resurgent and re-unified Hellenic world—had been resuscitated by Eleftherios Venizelos, this time as a kind of 'bourgeois revolution' of somewhat reduced dimensions after the Greek loss of Asia Minor. This 'revolution' was to be led by an educated, mercantile and professional class of Greek, and required great centres of appropriate education. Anargyros's school, based on the model of the British-style 'Public School', was to supply that need. The school was consciously to copy 'the model of Eton and Harrow'. The buildings, designed by George Diamantopoulos, were financed by legacies from both Anargyros and Marinos Koryialenios (d. 1910), a Greek merchant and banker based in London. The school was grandly conceived, with every facility including an observatory and an open-air theatre. When it opened in 1927, it had four students. In 1952/53 the novelist, John Fowles, taught at the school: his experiences were to underpin his novel ***The Magus*** eventually published in 1966. The 'Lord Byron School' on the 'Island of Phraxos', where the principal character, Nicholas Urfe, teaches, is based on the *Anargyreios and Koryialeneios* on Spetses. The school operated until its closure in 1983. The buildings are now used for international congresses and residential courses.

EAST FROM THE DAPIA TO THE OLD HARBOUR

Immediately east and one block in from the harbour mole, is the ***Plateia Rologiou*** ('Clock-tower Square'), an apology for a central square, with the **fish-market** on its north side, overlooked by the clock-tower of 1915. By weaving uphill from the south exit of the square, you come to the **Museum of Spetses** in the **Hadji-Yannis Mexis Mansion**, which lies five blocks inland from the shore. (*Open daily except Mon 8.30–2.30.*) The austere and imposing building—Genoese in concept, Ottoman in detail—dates from 1795–98; its design is very similar to the Koundouriotis and Gouroyannis mansions on Hydra which date from a little earlier, except that the arcaded loggia here rises from the ground through both floors, with a symmetrical arrangement of stairs to either side. In the centre of the courtyard, flanked by cannon, is the bust of Hadji-Yannis

Mexis (1756–1844), who had acquired the honorific prefix 'Hadji' after a pilgrimage to Jerusalem. As a respected elder of the island, he had been named 'Nazir of Spetses' by the Sultan in 1817. In 1821, he put his personal wealth and energies behind the Greek naval insurrection which began in Spetses.

The **museum** occupies the upper floor of the building, which consisted mostly of the women's quarters and guests' rooms: the spaces are simple and beautiful, but the collection is somewhat gloomily displayed. *Room I* exhibits maritime memorabilia; there are **ships' portraits** and some fine **figureheads**, as well as **archival photographs** of considerable interest.

The **archaeological material** is confined to *Room II*; it includes the earliest finds to have been made on the island, from the area immediately around the church of Aghia Marina where an Early Helladic II settlement of the 3rd millennium BC has been excavated. Note the fragment of the prow of a miniature boat. The other showcases are mostly occupied by the donation of a private collection (Kyros) which comprises a wide range of pieces from different ages and areas of Greece. The remarkably lustrous polish on the **black-glaze chalices** is particularly noteworthy. The centre of the room is occupied by a fine 4th century BC, **circular marble**

offering-table.

Rooms III, IV & V are dedicated to **ecclesiastical material, textiles, furniture** and **ceramics.** The latter illustrates the wide area of commercial contacts which Spetsiot traders had. An unusual piece is the **carved wooden icon** of Prophitis Elias in Room III. *Room VI*, which was the main reception room of the women's area, conserves the mortal **remains of Laskarina Bouboulina** in a casket. On the wall is the **revolutionary flag of Spetses**—a Greek cross surmounting the up-turned crescent moon, symbolising a subjugated Turkey.

Behind the museum building, 150m to the south are the evocative ruins of another grand mansion of similar design and comparable age, built by a member of the same family, Theodorakis Mexis, brother of Hadji-Yannis.

We return once again to the shore, and head east. At the end of the long sweep of the waterfront east of the Dapia, is a small promontory marked by the church of **Aghios Mamas.** On the shore-line stretch between here and the next promontory are a number of the finer stone **houses** of Spetses, mostly set up above high retaining walls. Similar in design, and yet subtly different; arranged in a line, but all at pleasingly differing angles; these simple yet dignified buildings are the expression of the island's economic prosperity and equitable distribution. They complement and frame the compound of the **monastery of Aghios Nikolaos**, the island's cathedral, which is set back above the next promontory to the east, with cannon emplacements on its seaward side. The complex is preceded by an esplanade of **pebble-mosaic pavement** with maritime figurative designs: it was in this open space that the uprising of Spetses was officially proclaimed at a meeting of the islanders on 3 April 1821, and that the revolutionary flag of the island was first hoisted on the bell-tower of the church. The tower and its carved elements are the work of marble craftsmen from Tinos.

Written sources for the foundation of the Monastery are lacking, but it must date from around the year 1700: the present, elegant complex of buildings is from a hundred years later. The catholicon is set at a very slight angle to the surrounding quadrangle. The builders have incorporated an unfinished fragment of **late Roman decorative frieze** in the wall above the west door, which still bears dense lines of perforations made with a running-drill; these would have been joined into a single flowing line with a chisel, if the piece had been completed. The interior is covered with recently executed, traditional iconographic painting and possesses a fine **wooden iconostasis** of c. 1805.

In 1827, Paul-Marie Bonaparte (1808–27), nephew of

Napoleon, was brought here by the frigate of Thomas Cochrane, which was on its way to the decisive encounter at
Navarino only six weeks later. The young Bonaparte (19
years old), who had come to fight in the Greek revolutionary war, was lodged in the monastery; he died shortly after
at Nauplia, and was buried on the western Peloponnesian
island of Sphacteria.

In rounding the promontory of Aghios Nikolaos, you enter the **bay of Baltiza**: the name comes from the Greek
word '*βάλτος*' meaning a shallow or marsh—a memory
of the fact that its upper (southern) reaches were originally just that. The deep cut in the coast and the protective headland to the east, however, destined it for use first
as a boat-yard, and then as a commercial harbour—the
'**Palaió Limáni**' or Old Harbour. Like Skiathos, and Symi,
Spetses had good supplies of pine-wood; it had access to
different hardwoods from the mainland, too, and it was
natural that the craft of boat-building should flourish
here. The tradition is not yet extinguished: amongst the
yachts and pleasure craft that crowd the harbour today
there are still small **yards dedicated to boat-building**,
and their activity is a source of fascination. It was from
the boat-builders of Spetses that Tim Severin, in the early
1980s, commissioned a reconstruction of a Bronze Age,

20-oar galley to replicate the kind of vessel that would have been used by the Argonauts on their search for the Golden Fleece through the Aegean and Black Sea waters. Today the harbour often seems clogged with small craft; but it should be recalled that, such was the size of the commercial fleet of Spetses in the first part of the 19th century, it was often possible to cross from one side of the inlet to the other on the fleets of ships moored side by side across its width. The contrast of the white, cubic buildings and the dark-green spires of cypress trees on the slopes which overlook the harbour is striking.

A pleasant walk can be made along the eastern promontory past the church of the **Panaghía Armáta**, which was built by the victorious Spetsiot naval commander, Ioannis Koutsis, who destroyed a part of the Turkish fleet in 1822 in the waters of the Gulf of Argos. Every year on 8 September there is a magnificent celebration of this victory in the bay of Baltiza, in which a vessel laden with fire-works, representing the Turkish flagship, blazes on the water. The path leads beyond to the **cannon-emplacements** and the **lighthouse**. The present '*Pharos*' dates from 1831 and was one of the first lighthouses of the independent Greek State.

AROUND THE ISLAND

INLAND OF THE SHORE

Some of the older churches of the town can be seen by following **Botasis Street** which leads uphill from the left-hand side of the Anargyros Mansion, behind the Dapia. Some of the older houses, to either side, have decorated marble panels inset in their façades: one example, in Baroque style, on the front of the **Botasis Mansion**, 250m up the street on the left, displays a medallion framed by deeply cut olive fronds. By descending to the right just beyond the three-apsed church of Aghios Giorgios, crossing the bridge below, and climbing again for 150m to the south, you come to the church of the **Koimisis tis Theotokou**, which functioned as the island's cathedral before the bishop's seat moved to Aghios Nikolaos. (*Generally open around 4pm for cleaning: otherwise key in house across dip to south of church.*) The exterior was decorated with inset ceramic dishes as trophies; many have been removed, but those around the apse remain. The interior which is of inscribed cross plan surmounted by a dome is attractively proportioned and luminous. Descending once again from here, towards the coast, you pass the church of the **Taxiarches** to the left and the large church of the **Aghia Triada** (1793) to the right of the street: both—as was frequently the case on Spetses—were built by rich Spetsiot merchants, Giorgios Economou and Emmanuel Papatheodorou respectively. In the neighbourhood are a number of the older houses and gardens of the town, some in ruins.

THE MONASTERY OF AGHII PANTES, AND AROUND THE ISLAND

Aghii Pantes, the Monastery of All Saints (*a 20-minute walk to the south of the town, reached by continuing uphill from the museum*), is a peaceful and immaculate convent of 6 nuns, dating from the beginning of the last century, overlooking the town and the south and east coasts. The monastery's main *icon of the Aghii Pantes* is unusual and has the appearance of a *mandala*; beneath the great circle of saints sit Abraham, Isaac and Jacob in paradise, with the souls of the good in their laps. The interior is plain except for paintings around the sanctuary arch. To the south side of the *catholicon* is the unusual **pyramidal sepulchre**, in grey stone, of Dionysios Goudis, benefactor and member of one of the maritime families of the island.

The **view** from the monastery to the east, with the

contrasting forms and colours of the cypresses, olives and red-tiled roofs shelving to the sea, the island of Spetsopoula opposite, and Hydra and Dokos in the distance, is delightful. Visible below on the coast is the small church of **Aghia Marina**, which is reached by following the main road south out of the town and turning left just at the edge of habitation. The church is at the tip of a small projection of land with bays to either side: this configuration—two harbours and a rudimentarily fortifiable promontory—gave rise to habitation in earliest times. Excavations around the church have revealed the existence of a substantial settlement of the mid-3rd millennium BC (Early Helladic II), whose pottery finds, now in the Spetses Museum, show contacts with the mainland and the Cyclades. There are traces of later Mycenaean habitation on the site as well.

South of Aghia Marina the coast road passes a number of large estates, purchased by members of some of the wealthiest and most important, Greek shipping families— Lemos and Niarchos. **Spetsópoula** (Ancient *Aristera*), the pine-forested island offshore to the east, was purchased in 1962 by Stavros Niarchos. Several other Athenian business magnates have built estates further along the shore; in summer the waters are filled with the conspicuous, private yachts of yet others, drawn to the island by plutocratic magnetism. The landscape beyond, however, is contrastingly destitute. Repeated forest fires through the 1990s and especially in the summer of 2000, have left the south coast of the island and its interior charred and scalded, a tragedy that has not even spared the once idyllic coves of **Aghia Paraskevi**, and **Aghii Anargyri**, with its famous shoreside canopied **grotto**. A small patch of forest, of Niarchos property, close to the bay of Zogeriá has survived, but otherwise the landscape is denuded and will take many decades to restore fully. Arriving after nearly 30km at the north shore once again, the trees return. The delightful inlet of **Ligonéri** (just outside the northwestern extremity of the town), reminds one of the beauty of the combination of pines and rocks and water which made Spetses so famous.

PRACTICAL INFORMATION

180 50 **Spétses** or, more formally, **Spétsai**: area 20sq. km; perimeter 31km; resident population 3,772; max. altitude 245m. **Port Authority**: T. 22980 72245. **Travel and information**: Spetses Travel, T. 22980 73400, www.spetses.gr

ACCESS

By boat: In addition to an (all-weather) car and passenger ferry which runs daily from Piraeus to Spetses in summer, and 5 times weekly in the winter, Spetses has typically 3 connections a day by Hydrofoil and three by fast Catamaran, which ply the route from Piraeus to Spetses via Poros, Hydra and Ermioni, and on to Porto Heli. All these vessels are run by *Hellenic Seaways* (www.hellenicseaways.gr). For the reduced services of the faster vessels between mid-October and Easter, which can sometimes be suspended in bad weather, it is best to visit the company's web-site. The 15-min crossing from Kosta on the mainland opposite Spetses is made by the car-ferry, *Katerina Star*, 4 times daily, leaving Kosta at 8, 10.30, 1.20 and 5. **Note**: *private cars belonging to non-residents on the island are not allowed on Spetses.*

LODGING

Since the closure of Spetses' historic **Hotel Poseidonion** for renovation, the luxury end of the scale is represented by the rather sterile facilities of the **Nissia Traditional Residences** on the water front, west of Dapia: the residences are not 'traditional', but modern luxury apartments (*T. 22980 75000–10, fax 75012, www.nissia.gr*). Slightly further west on the sea front is the **Archontiko Economou**, providing all comforts in a restored, traditional Spetsiot house of 1851 (*T. 22980 73400, fax 74074, www. spetsesyc.gr/economoumansion. htm*). Simple but comfortable accommodation (medium price) is offered at the **Hotel Roumani** at Dapia (*T. 22980 72244, fax 73061, www.hotel-roumani.gr*). These last two are open year-round.

EATING

Two traditional tavernas stand out; the fish taverna, **Patralis**, at the western end of Spetses town in Kounoupitsa, is welcoming with good service and delicious fish dishes, amongst which is the typical '*psari á la Spetsiotika*'. 200m up Botasis Street from the Anargyros Mansion, **Lazaros Taverna**, behind the church of Aghios Giorgios, is one of the few traditional, neighbourhood tavernas surviving in the town. Fresh goat's-milk yoghurt and a variety of natural products can be bought at '**Mandragorás**' store, close to the clock tower.

INDEX